CRATE

DIGGER

Crate Digger

An Obsession With Punk Records

Bob Suren
First Printing, June 9, 2015
All text is © Bob Suren, 2015
This edition is © Microcosm Publishing, 2015
Photos as individually credited

In the Punk History series

Microcosm Publishing
2752 N Williams Ave
Portland, OR 97227

For a catalog, write or visit
MicrocosmPublishing.com

ISBN 978-1-62106-878-5
This is Microcosm #193

Distributed worldwide by Legato / Perseus
and in England by Turnaround

Edited by Joe Biel and Lauren Hage
Designed by Joe Biel
Cover by Meggyn Pomerleau

This book was printed on post-consumer paper by union workers in
the United States.

CRATE

DIGGER

An Obsession
With Punk Records

CONTENTS

Introduction..6

Where: 3421...7

7 Seconds *Skins, Brains, & Guts*.....................8

All You Can Eat *With Salad Bar*.....................10

Where: 113-H East Brandon Blvd......................14

Ataque Frontal *s/t*................................16

B-52s *Wild Planet*.................................21

Bad Brains *Rock for Light*.........................22

Bad Posture *s/t*...................................24

Who: Brian R. and Kevin.............................27

Who: Ella...30

Black Flag *Jealous Again*..........................33

Cult Ritual *s/t*...................................35

Dead Boys *Young, Loud, and Snoty*..................39

Dead Kennedys *Fresh Fruit for Roting Vegetables*...42

Where: PO Box 3204..................................45

Dictators *Go Girl Crazy!*..........................46

Disorderly Conduct *Amen*...........................48

Who: Sam and Pete...................................52

D.O.A. *Hardcore '81*...............................55

Drills *Certificate of Penetration*.................57

Eat *Communist Radio/Catholic Love*.................59

F *You Are An E.P.*.................................60

F *Four From '84*...................................64

Failure Face *s/t*..................................68

Flaming Midget *Midget Melodies: Very Short songs for the
Very Short*...71

Flipper *Generic Flipper*...........................77

Gay Cowboys in Bondage *Owen Marshmallow Strikes Again*..78

Gross National Product *Ronald McVomit's 14 Song Happy Meal*
....82

Who: Pat and Brian L................................86

Gun Club *Fire of Love*.............................89

Hated Youth *Hardcore Rules*........................91

MDC *Millions of Dead Cops*.........................93

Meatmen *We're The Meatmen...And You Suck!*.........96

Minor Threat *Out of Step*.........................100

Misfits *Die, Die, My Darling*............................*102*
Misfits *Walk Among Us*...................................*105*
Negative Approach s/t....................................108
Pillsbury Hardcore *In A Straightedge Limbo*....,,,,,,....*110*
Ramones *It's Alive*......................................*112*
Who: Edgar and Oliver....................................117
Rattus *Uskonto on Vara*..................................*119*
Raw Power *Screams from The Gutter*.......................*122*
Reason of Insanity s/t...................................127
Richard Hell and the Voidoids *Blank Generation*........*130*
Sex Pistols *Never Mind The Bollocks*.....................*132*
Slap of Reality *Stuck Inside*............................*133*
Sorto *Aina Valmiina*.....................................*136*
Stalin *Go Go Stalin*.....................................*139*
Television *Marquee Moon*.................................*141*
Terrorain *1988 Demos*....................................*142*
Toxic Reasons *Kill by Remote Control*...................146
Varaus *1/2*..*150*
VKTMS *Midget*..*152*
Where: 203...154
Where: Unit 49-B...160
Where: Egypt and Ecuador.................................165
Young Wasteners *We Got Ways*.............................*169*
Where: The Independent...................................171
Various Artists *A Compilation Dedicated to Tim Yohannan*.*172*
Various Artists *Frank Forever*...........................*175*
Various Artists *Grito Suburbano*.....................,,,,,,,*180*
Various Artists *Let Them Eat Jellybeans*................*184*
Various Artists *We Can't Help It If We're From Florida*.....*186*
Epilogue...188

DEDICATED TO all the people who were part of my life in music, to my heroes and friends, to the people who worked and played beside me in good times and bad. To Ella who let me live my dreams. And to June, who remains out of reach.

INTRODUCTION

I spent 30 years of my life consumed by punk rock music. At first I was just a listener but quickly got caught up in the excitement of it all. I began playing in bands, writing about music, and shooting photos. I published my own magazine and edited another. I hosted 35 record conventions. I ran the Burrito Records label and Sound Idea, a record distribution and store, for eighteen, sixteen, and fourteen years, respectively. I contributed to four books. I had a syndicated Internet radio show. I had a bootleg music merchandising empire. I promoted more than 600 concerts and traveled all over with my own music.

I began collecting records, a pursuit with no end. I saw each record as a piece of a fascinating puzzle. With each piece, the picture became more detailed. Each piece brought deeper understanding of this genre, its history and its ideologies. I amassed several thousand pieces of vinyl plus who knows how many cassettes and CDs. I also had books, magazines, posters, videos, and other items of ephemera. My living room looked like a record store. It wasn't enough. I always wanted to do more. I wanted bigger projects and more records. Always more records.

With the music came travel, friendships, assholes, hard work, satisfaction and disappointment. And I found the person I fell in love with.

This book is a patchwork of memories, profiling some of the most important records in my life. This book is like a long conversation between two friends in a room full of records. I'm glad you're here with me, friend.

WHERE: 3421

3421 is the house my parents built in Stuart, Florida in 1979. I lived there until I went to college. After college, I lived there for a few more years, saving money and figuring out what to do with myself.

3421 is where I first heard many of my favorite bands on vinyl and cassette tapes. 3421 is where I started my record label and where the label grew into a mail order distribution company. Lots of nights I was up late, pecking away on an old typewriter, putting together my first mail order catalogs. One night my mom asked me to stop clacking the keys of the typewriter at 2 AM so she could get some sleep. I didn't sleep much then.

3421 is where I started my own music magazine. By then I had a computer and the clicking of the keys was much quieter.

The town was too small and I was going crazy there. By the time I left, I was past ready to leave; I didn't much care when my parents sold the place in summer 2012.

Me with one of my first bands at the Downtown Club, April 1986, Stuart, FL. Photographer unknown.

7 SECONDS
SKINS, BRAINS AND GUTS 7"
ALTERNATIVE TENTACLES 1982

7 Seconds was my favorite band for a few years. They took the ball from the pioneering Minor Threat and ran with it. I collected all of the 7 Seconds stuff.

An older guy in my high school got into American hardcore as soon as it happened. He was Year One and I was like Year Three. He loaned out and taped lots of records for people. His copy of *Skins, Brains, and Guts* made the rounds at school. When it finally dropped into my hands, I fell in love with not just the raw, urgent sounds on the record but the raw, urgent graphics on the cover. Everything about this record screamed, "HARDCORE!" It is one of the finest examples of the genre. And it made me feel like I was part of something really cool.

Like a lot of Year One guys, he eventually proclaimed hardcore dead and began giving away all of his records. I ended up with his copy of *Skins, Brains, and Guts* and the first MDC album. I blasted both of these over and over like high-decibel mantras.

7 Seconds released the *Committed for Life* 7" next, but no copies made it to our small circle for a few years. The next 7 Seconds my friends and I heard was their first full length, *The Crew.*

My pal Mike bought *The Crew* and hated it because it sounded nothing like *Skins, Brains, and Guts.* Had we heard *Committed,* the transition would have been less of a shock. And so I ended up with Mike's copy of *The Crew.* I gave him a D.O.A. record, which I found slow and boring.

This was the first time I traded records and it felt weird. Not like I was getting ripped off, but like I wasn't sure it was something I was supposed to do. My parents raised me to take care of my possessions and although they never said anything, I got the feeling that they would not want me to trade my stuff. But by then I was a certified punk rocker, trying all kinds of new things that my parents would not approve of.

I took an immediate liking to *The Crew.* It was different from the band I fell in love with, but I accepted it. Over the years, 7 Seconds changed sounds a few times; I tried to keep up with them, but I never liked the later era of the band. *The Crew* became a melodic code of conduct for me and thousands of people around the world. Their positive, profound lyrics coupled with electric playing pulled me in. I quickly memorized the lyrics and still know them.

A year later, 7 Seconds followed up with the *Walk Together, Rock Together* 12" EP. I was at a record store, standing in line, when the UPS guy dropped off a big box on the sales counter. The clerk asked me if I could wait until he opened the box. Right on top was *Walk Together.*

"I never saw that one before!"

"It's the new record, produced by Ian MacKaye." I didn't know what "produced" meant, but I knew Ian MacKaye was the singer of Minor Threat, one of my favorite bands.

"Uh... Can I buy one?"

"Sure, just let me make sure everything is here first."

So I put back whatever was in my hands and waited for the clerk to check inventory. He sold me the top copy from the box, the one I first laid eyes on. I was about to walk out the door, marveling at an all-new, super cool 7 Seconds record, when he stopped me and asked if we could listen to it.

We broke it out of the plastic and plopped it on the store's turntable. And we were both immediately floored. After we listened to the whole thing—it is less than eighteen minutes—he called a friend and said, "Hey, have you heard the new 7 Seconds? It's really good. You want me to hold a copy?"

That was 1985, the year that 7 Seconds become a phenomenon. Two weeks after this came out I was at a concert in Miami. Between bands, the club played the entire record over the P.A. system; the whole crowd sang every word louder than the record on the P.A.

ALL YOU CAN EAT
WITH SALAD BAR 7"
WIMP RECORDS 1991

Our band Failure Face drove all through the night, from Augusta, Georgia to Milwaukee, Wisconsin, to meet up with All You Can Eat. Rob Sexton, our drummer, told me that there were times when touring would not be fun. This was one of them. It was boring and cramped, but playing at the end of the day made everything better. It was my first tour, the summer of 1993.

We got a flat tire somewhere in southern Illinois while going 75 mph. Fortunately it was a back tire and we didn't lose control of our well-aged Ford Econoline. Jim the roadie was driving at the time. We didn't have a jack, so Kevin stood on the side of the road with a cardboard sign that read, "WE NEED A JACK," and eventually a good guy pulled over and helped our stupid, young asses.

We didn't have a jack because when we'd packed the van a week earlier at Rob's house in Tampa, there was not room for everything and something had to be left behind. Rob said we didn't need the jack. I thought that was a bad idea, but it just did not fit. Rob said, "We probably won't need it anyway," adding that by merely having a jack on board we would be inviting trouble. So, we didn't have a jack.

Rob had toured many times. Jim had been on a few tours, too. Brian R., Kevin and I had never toured before, so we listened to Rob and Jim. Jim is now a professional road manager with popular bands, touring on big buses and planes, eating deli platters and staying in hotels. He's come a long way from our Ford Econoline days.

The day before we left on tour, we gave the van an oil change and painted it with white house paint, using brushes and paint rollers, in Rob's front yard. One time we were caught in a sudden downpour on I-95 just outside of Richmond, Virginia. It was weather of Biblical intensity and it came out of nowhere. Rob flipped on the windshield wipers and after about five swipes, they stopped in the middle of the windshield. We lost visibility in one second and clearly we were going to die. Brian R., who was riding shotgun, let out an ape-like yell and punched the dashboard. The wipers came back on. It was a punk rock miracle.

So, we borrowed a damn jack and put on our bald spare. I told Rob that we should get a new tire as soon as possible and he said, "We don't have money for that," adding that the odds of getting *another* flat were pretty slim. We finished the tour on that bald tire. Somehow we got to Milwaukee with extra time.

The gig was at a neighborhood bar called Quarters in a gritty part of town, though all of Milwaukee looked gritty. All You Can Eat, our tour partners for the next two weeks, were already there. Rob and Jim knew them from previous road days. Introductions were made: Devon, Myron, Danny, and Craig, California guys who still travel all over the world with their music.

Before tour, Rob said that All You Can Eat was a popular band and that playing with them would get more people to see us. All You Can Eat are great guys and a fun band, but Rob had greatly overestimated their drawing power. Case in point, Muncie, Indiana.

We raced All You Can Eat to Muncie, they in their tan Volkswagen micro-bus and we in the white-house painted Econoline. We'd split from them for a day to hang out in Chicago. But as we were rolling across the open Midwest, their van appeared out of nowhere and blew past us, blowing the horn, a couple of middle fingers extended from the windows.

"Get those fuckers," Rob yelled and Brian R. gunned the Econoline. There was much flinger flipping, ass-baring, and the throwing of old food between the two vans, all at ludicrous speed. We beat the Californians by a few minutes, pulling up to the venue several hours early. It was a place called the Dead Pigeon Café.

We had hours before show time, so our two bands walked around Muncie in search of something to do. This place looked whipped. After walking for ten minutes without seeing anything interesting, I spotted what looked like a real punk rocker. It was a hot, July afternoon but he was wearing a leather jacket. On the back, he'd painted, "Muncie Hardcore Crew" in huge, white letters. Muncie Hardcore Crew! We ran up to him to talk.

He knew about the show and planned to be there. I asked him about the Muncie Hardcore Crew, specifically, how many people were in it. He smiled, pointed his thumb at his chest and said, "Just me." A crew of one. Muncie was not looking promising.

The Muncie Hardcore Crew guy came to the show as promised. He and four other people (who presumably were not in the Crew) attended. There was also a local band. I don't remember their name, but when All You Can Eat was playing, the local band threw firecrackers at them, called them faggots, and ran away.

To top it off, the club had the world's most ineffective doorman. He was sitting at the door, supposedly to collect money, but he never took a dollar from anyone. He didn't even ask. The five audience members walked by like he wasn't even there. I pointed this out to the owner who was some burned out hippie. He told me to "cool out" and that we'd be taken care of. At the end of the night, he gave me twenty dollars. It was for both bands. Rob told me there'd be nights like these.

But there were awesome nights, too, like our last night on the road with All You Can Eat in Gulfport, Mississippi. That summer there was serious flooding in Alabama and Mississippi. When we got to Gulfport, most of the main streets were closed off due to flooding. The National Guard was re-directing traffic.

The show was in a rental hall, a VFW or a Lion's Club. The parking lot was full of people waiting to see a concert, standing patiently in the rain. When our van pulled in, the crowd cheered. They didn't know who we were, but we were the first band to show up. We jumped out of the van into shin-deep water. It was going to be a sloppy night, no doubt about that.

Needless to say, the die-hard music fans, the bored youth of Gulfport, went completely mental for every band that night. And they bought merchandise. Afterward, the locals followed us and All You Can Eat to a Waffle House, where we dined together for the last time, exchanged phone numbers and hugs. All You Can Eat hopped into their Volkswagen and headed west on I-10. We hopped into the white house-painted Econoline and headed east, back to Florida.

Myron of All You Can Eat at Blue Chair Music, Halloween
1994 in Tampa. Photo by Bob Suren

WHERE: 113-H EAST BRANDON BLVD.

I opened up my record shop in 1995, naming it Sound Idea. I spent so much time there that it became like a person to me. We had a relationship. If you've lived or worked somewhere for a long time, you know what I mean.

I lived at Sound Idea for a while, until my landlord found out and threatened to evict me. I had a small futon that someone gave me. I kept my clothing in a few plastic crates under a table. I shaved and showered at the gym down the street. Even when I moved out, I was there so much that it was more of a home than my house. I was comfortable there. I walked around in my socks and took most of my meals there. When no one else was around, I'd talk out loud, voicing my joy or my boredom or my frustration to the walls. I cried there a few times. I laughed there many more. I passed fourteen years there, seven days a week, ten to fourteen hours a day.

One time my landlord wanted me to switch units so he could tear down the walls between 113-H and 113-I to create a bigger space. I wouldn't move.

At first I thought the shop would be strictly a commercial venture. But I put down roots. It became a community meeting place and the hub of our local music scene. Friendships were made, bands were formed, and a handful of people fell in love there, including me. I wanted to get married there, but she didn't.

The first few years at Sound Idea were a breeze. The money came in so easily that I couldn't believe it. It seemed like a dream job. I used to laugh when I unlocked the door every morning. I privately called it the Money Factory until around 2001, when sales started dipping. Each year they got a little worse. I figured I could ride it out until business got back to normal, but it never even got close.

By 2008, I couldn't keep it running any longer; I told those closest to me first and asked them to keep it a secret until I was ready to make a public announcement. After I broke the news, one of my musical heroes, Jello Biafra, the singer of the Dead Kennedys, called to tell me how sorry he was. He had visited 113-H a few years earlier. Losing the record store was like a death in the family. It is still hard to talk about.

Some of the people I met there became lifelong friends. Others I'll never see again. I don't know all of their names, but at least once a week since closing, someone will tell me how important the place was. I always smile and thank them.

The last day in business was a cross between a family reunion and a wake. I went out of business with an all-night concert by multiple local bands. Hundreds of people showed up, faces from the last fourteen years. That night, I slept there alone for the last time.

SOUND IDEA
RECORDS-CD'S-CASSETTES
653-2550

RECORDS

SOUND IDEA ONLY

SOUND IDEA ONLY

First week of business, March 1995. Photo by Bob Suren

ATAQUE FRONTAL
S/T 7"
NEW WAVE RECORDS 1986

By the late 1980s, people were proclaiming hardcore punk dead. Most of these people were Americans. I was not one of these people. I understand how those focused on U.S. hardcore could get this impression. By 1986, all of the first wave U.S. bands were broken up or had changed their styles considerably. Bands either got wimpy or went speed metal. The so-called youth crew genre was exploding, which alienated a lot of people, including me.

Fortunately, as hardcore waned in America, it was in full stride elsewhere. I started picking up on international hardcore in 1985 or so. At first I collected German hardcore as it was plentiful and easy to find. Then I started hearing bands from Finland, Sweden, Italy, and other far-off places that made the Germans sound tame. Around 1989 or 1990, I got my first tastes of South American hardcore and the game changed again.

I ordered the Ataque Frontal 7" expressly because the band was from Peru. I vaguely knew where Peru was on the map. What, I wondered, would Peruvian hardcore sound like? Three bucks and a couple of weeks later, I found out. The Ataque Frontal 7" was easily the angriest record I'd ever experienced, especially Silvio's vocals—DAMN! I played it and copied it at least twenty times for the uninitiated. They were all quickly won over.

Ataque Frontal made it onto just about every mix tape I constructed for the next several years. A lot of people had never heard them. I was bummed out that it was so hard to find. I started thinking about reissuing it if I could find the band or record label. The idea kicked around in my head for a few years. In 2003 I fired off a letter to New Wave Records, addressed to the contact info on the back of the original record from 1986. What were the odds of the label still having the same address seventeen years later? I had nothing to lose but a stamp.

I got a response a few months later. Unfortunately, the label turned down my request for a reissue as they had planned to do it. That was fine with me. As long as it was coming back out, I was happy. Two years later, the reissue had not materialized so I wrote back to New Wave, reaffirming my request. This time, permission was granted. Now I needed to find the band.

I wrote another letter. This one was sent to the band address from the original record. Nineteen years had passed since the record came out. Astoundingly, my letter landed in the hands of guitarist José Eduardo Matute.

José told me I could reissue the record if I paid him five hundred dollars. I explained that my label, Burrito Records, was very small and that five hundred dollars would greatly affect the price per unit of the 1,000 records I planned for the first pressing. I broke down the price structure for him to show that there was not room in the budget. I instead offered him 100 copies of the record. He told me he didn't need 100 records and again asked for five hundred dollars. When I told him that much money was out of the question, he basically told me to fuck off.

I felt dejected, but it was a financial impossibility, so I let the matter drop. A few weeks later, José emailed to say he could settle for less money. And negotiations began. I kept pushing to pay him in records, he kept pushing for money. Eventually we reached a compromise. I think I paid him three hundred dollars and 30 copies of the record. It was the only time in the history of my record label that a band asked for money. I was not happy about it, but we made a deal. I sent the money by Western Union. A few months later, the record was out and José got his 30 copies.

My reissue contained an extra song and expanded packaging. I grabbed the extra song from a compilation album that José forgot all about. I didn't tell him that I intended to add the extra song because I didn't want him asking for more money. I just put it on there and thankfully, he was pleasantly surprised. He told me he really liked my version.

The first pressing sold out fast. I did a second pressing of 1,000 copies, helping me offset the three hundred dollar royalty payment. My relationship with José improved. He was happy to see the record back out and getting good reviews.

Before the band was called Ataque Frontal, they were called Guerrilla Urbana and did many of the same songs. An early version of Guerrilla Urbana had a different singer who was way less intense. I asked José if there were any Guerrilla Urbana recordings. Yes, he told me, there were two recording sessions, one with the first singer and one with Silvio, the angriest singer on earth. I asked if I could hear the recordings and maybe reissue them. New negotiations began. I booked a flight to Lima.

In Lima, José picked me up at my hotel room and we went out to eat at a Chinese-Peruvian restaurant. Over dinner we discussed Peru, the U.S., and music. Toward the end of dinner, José passed the Guerrilla Urbana master tapes to me across the table. I hoped they were recorded and preserved well, as they dated back to 1985.

José's job was working as a documentary filmmaker for the Peruvian government. He made films about Peruvian history and culture. He offered to show me around Lima for a couple of days. I could not have asked for a better tour guide.

We walked around Lima and he pointed out the important sights. His knowledge was impressive. It was obvious he was proud of his city. As we walked by a monastery, an old priest greeted us on the sidewalk. He and José began speaking rapidly in Spanish. I understood very little of the conversation. Finally José turned to me and asked, "Would you like a tour of the monastery?"

The priest took us around the monastery, explaining when it was built and what the various rooms were used for. He explained that there was a series of secret tunnels running under the monastery that went all over Lima. José translated all this for me, as the priest spoke no English. At the conclusion of the tour, José and the priest started arguing about something. José said something in pissed-off Spanish and made a dramatic hand gesture. The priest yelled something at him in Spanish as José dragged me away.

"What was that all about?"

Turns out the tour was not free. The priest wanted money and José told him to fuck off.

Next José took me to a museum. He told me it was free. But when we got to the entrance, he got into another argument with the doorman and again, he dragged me off.

Turns out the museum is only free to Peruvians. The doorman wanted to charge me ten dollars for being American. I told José that I was fine with paying, but he insisted this was unfair and that I should boycott the museum on principle.

That evening we went to a rock club to watch a few bands. A Flock of Seagulls had played there recently; there was a promo photo on the wall. Unfortunately, the bands playing that night were not very good. Sensing I wasn't having a good time, José proposed going to a record store instead. It was about 1:00 in the morning. There was a record store open at 1:00 in the morning? OK, let's go.

We walked down some very sketchy streets. A lot of people called out and waved to José. I am pretty sure that if he was not with me, I might have been in trouble, but in his company, nobody messed with me.

At the record store, José knocked on a huge iron door with one of those sliding eye-hole things that you see in old detective movies. It slid open and a pair of eyes appeared in the slot. The eyes recognized José. Then the eyes looked me over. The thing slid shut and the door cracked open. Apparently this was a top-secret record shop. When I walked in, I saw why.

There were people doing all kinds of drugs all over the place. People were snorting, smoking, and injecting who knows what. I was a little uncomfortable, but I wanted to do some record shopping, so it was off to the racks. The druggies barely noticed us.

I quickly surmised that everything in the record shop was bootleg: CDs, DVDs, cassettes, t-shirts, patches, stickers, and pins, all unauthorized reproductions. There was no vinyl. I didn't recognize anything on the racks, but I'm a curious guy. I asked José to help me pick out something good.

He went straight to the CDs and picked out a self-titled disc by Los Saicos, a Peruvian band from 1965.

"This is my favorite album," José said in a very measured tone. With his endorsement, I picked it up. When I finally got around to playing it, I was blown away. Like Ataque Frontal, this one was a certified rocker and I ended up copying it plenty of times for people I like.

The next day we were on a bus and I asked José about New Wave Records. He went into a rant about how they ripped off the band and how that guy could fuck off. But he told me that I treated him fairly and he was very happy to be working with me again.

A couple of months later, I was back in Florida, beginning work on Guerrilla Urbana. I listened to the music and picked out the songs I wanted to use. José had very different opinions about which songs to use. I feel that he picked some of the weaker songs and ignored some obvious ragers. But he insisted on his selections. The record would not be as strong as it could be, but at least it was coming out.

I took the music to Audio Lab Studios in Tampa. With the help of pro sound engineer Josh Young we made those old tapes sound better than ever. I sent José the restored music and he was very happy. At this point I asked him to send me photos and images of the band that I could use for the cover and inside packaging.

He told me that a friend of his was designing the packaging with a fancy computer program. My heart sank. I wanted this raw, 1980s Peruvian hardcore record to look like a raw, 1980s Peruvian hardcore record. I hate clean computer layouts. I begged him to let me do the packaging but he would not budge.

I relented. I told him to make sure that his friend did the layouts the correct size and in black and white. I did not have the money in my budget for color packaging. I also pleaded to have his friend design the art with paper, scissors, and glue so it would have the right look.

A week later, I received a computer disc in an overnight DHL package from Peru. I popped the disc into my computer. The layouts were the wrong size, they were in full color, and they looked like something from a nu metal album.

I emailed José to tell him I could not use the layouts. Again I asked him to let me do the art my way. He not only refused, he told me that I owed him sixty five dollars for the overnight delivery. I never asked for the stuff to be sent overnight. Still, he wanted his money. I told him I wouldn't pay and no longer wanted to do the project. Characteristically, he told me to fuck off. That was the last I heard from him. I offered the project to another label and explained the situation. The other guy didn't want to touch it.

Four or five years later, I was standing in line at the Brandon Post Office, flipping through the latest issue of *Maximum Rocknroll*, and a small article caught my eye. It was a brief obituary for José Eduardo Matute. The article was scant on details. I contacted a few people who might have more info and skimmed the Internet but I couldn't find a thing. I'm not sure how he died. I think he was 46.

Guerrilla Urbana was recently reissued by another label. And I am glad that I was able to give Ataque Frontal a new life for a couple of years.

B-52S
WILD PLANET LP
WARNER BROTHERS 1980

When I was in middle school, a couple of years before I caught the punk rock bug, bands like Devo and the B-52s gave me the vague feeling that there was something more happening in music than arena rock. This other music was far stranger than Foreigner and Styx and I was far stranger than my peers.

At middle school dances, the weird kids would wait all night for the hired DJ to play either "Whip It" or "Rock Lobster," screaming the song titles out every ten minutes or so just in case the dude was deaf or had a very short term memory or something.

The DJ would always smile and say, "Later on, later on." This went on for hours. He always waited until the last song or two of the night to honor our mutant requests and then we'd dance like mental patients, especially during the "Down, down..." part of "Rock Lobster."

Well, one night the DJ blew our minds by playing "Strobe Light," an even stranger song that none of us except a super-cool girl named Laura had ever heard, and it was the greatest spaz-out ever.

BAD BRAINS
ROCK FOR LIGHT LP
PVC RECORDS 1983

My first car was a red 1964 Chevy with a tape deck. I had a tape with the Bad Brains on one side and the Freeze on the other. Back then I used to like picking up hitchhikers. It was cheap entertainment and marginally humanitarian.

My family had a tradition of getting pizza every Friday. It gave my mom a break from cooking and it was a nice way to start the weekend. I usually drove up to get the pizza.

The pizza place was about one mile from our house. One Friday as I was driving back with the pie, listening to my Bad Brains tape, I saw a hitchhiker wearing what I thought was a Bad Brains shirt. I knew I had to pull over.

Back then, especially in a small town, punk rockers were uncommon. If you saw someone in a band T-shirt, you had a secret connection. Seeing a stranger in a Bad Brains shirt was cause for jubilation. A fellow punk rocker. A Bad Brains fan in my town that I didn't know. I pulled over so fast and so close to the guy that I scared him.

It wasn't a Bad Brains shirt. The guy wasn't a punk rocker. He was homeless. Sometimes it is hard to tell the punk rockers from the homeless.

There are not many homeless people in Stuart. They are more uncommon than punk rockers. So, he was a curiosity. He was also in need of some help—and he was already in my car—so I asked him, "Where are you heading?"

This stumped him. He was hitchhiking but had no destination in mind. He probably didn't think anyone would ever pick him up. He paused to consider and then said, "I don't know. How's the beach?"

"Beach is great here."

"Then I'll go to the beach. Hey, is that pizza?"

Yes, pizza. I offered him a slice. He grabbed one and took a big, first bite. The Bad Brains were still on the stereo.

"Hey, who's this?" he asked, tilting his head slightly toward the tape deck.

"The Bad Brains."

"The Bad Brains," he repeated, evaluating both the name and the music, "That's cool."

We headed toward the beach, talking a little and listening to the Bad Brains. He finished off the slice well before we got there. I pulled into a parking spot to let him out and wished him luck.

"Hey, did you say the Bad Brains? I have to remember that. Hey, can I have another piece of pizza?"

I let him grab another slice. He thanked me and he headed toward the boardwalk.

When I got home, my dad wanted to know what the hell took so long and why were there two pieces missing.

BAD POSTURE
S/T 12"
IRRESPONSIBLE RECORDS 1983

One of the good things about running a record store is that I got first dibs on everything that came in used. My first few years in business were a bonanza for used vinyl and my collection grew exponentially. After that, the local supply dried up and the used stuff came in dribs and drabs.

People had different reasons for selling their records. Sometimes they just didn't like the stuff anymore. Sometimes they had multiple copies. One nice guy needed money for a ski trip with his family.

One guy needed money to get divorced and move back to California. A couple of times people needed money for drugs.

There was a drug guy who had good records. Word was that he stole many of them. I don't know that for sure; it was just grapevine talk. A couple of times he came in to sell me records, a few pieces at a time. He did have good records, but they were usually beat to shit.

In record collecting, condition is very important. His record were always scuffed and scratched. The covers were always bent up and dingy. A few of the covers had cigarette burns and food stains. If the record was supposed to have an insert, it was missing. If it wasn't missing, it was probably dog-eared. In his hands, hundred-dollar records became twenty-dollar records. I once asked this guy if he kept his records in a gravel pit in the back yard. He didn't understand.

One day the drug guy told me he wanted to sell everything. I checked my cash reserve. I had about three hundred dollars. It would not be enough to buy everything, but I told him to come in. An hour later, the guy showed up with seven or eight boxes of records. It was maybe a thousand pieces. There was no way I had enough money for everything.

The guy was tense and shaky. His eyes were red. He was either stoned or going through withdrawals. He paced the store while I sorted through his stuff. Much of it was in bad shape, too common or already in stock. I went for the best stuff first, checking conditions as I went.

As I pulled out each record that I wanted, I held it up for him to see and told him what I could pay for it. He was not even paying attention. I could have been saying anything. I could have been speaking German.

"I can give you five for this."

"OK."

"Ten for this one."

"OK."

"This one is beat, so the best I can do is about seven bucks."

"Alright."

I added up the items on my calculator as I called out each price. He never disputed the prices. I made very fair offers. He had the Bad Posture 12", a heavy collector piece, and it was not in bad shape at all. I put that one aside for myself. When the total hit three dollar hundred, I had to stop.

I told him, "I can give you three hundred dollars for this stuff." It was about forty items.

"What about the rest?"

I explained that I was out of money and that I had to pass on the other stuff. I told him that if he came back in a few days, I might be able to get a few more things, but really, the rest was crap.

"Give me four hundred for everything."

He had about 900 records left. He was willing to throw them all in for another hundred bucks. He must have needed drugs really bad. If I had the extra hundred, I would have done it, but I just didn't have it.

"All I have is three hundred. If you come back in a few days, I can take a few more. "

"How about three hundred and fifty dollars for everything right now?"

Man, he was desperate. I told him I didn't have another dollar to spend. I really didn't. He took the three hundred bucks and loaded the rest of his records back into his car, mumbling under his breath the whole time. He didn't even bother to look at what I bought.

I got to work cleaning and pricing the records. I kept about a dozen things for myself. I put the others out in the store and called a couple of local collectors to tell them that I just made a score. One guy showed up and bought two or three things right away.

A couple of hours later, the phone rang. It was the drug guy.

"Uh, what all did you get from me?"

I started naming off some of the titles. He was shocked.

"What? I would have never sold that! How much did you give me for that?"

I couldn't recall every price. There were about forty items. I gave him ballpark figures.

"What? That record is worth way more than that!"

He complained about every item I named. Finally I stopped naming items and prices and reminded him that he agreed to each price as I called it out. I also reminded him that he was willing to sell me everything for three hundred and fifty dollars.

Seller's remorse. He wanted his records back. Of course he no longer had the money and I had already sold a few.

"Man, you ripped me off!"

I hoped those drugs were really good, because I had his records.

WHO: BRIAN R. AND KEVIN

My friend Rob and I wanted to start a band. He met Brian R. and decided that he'd be perfect. In 1992 I took Rob's opinions as if they were carved in granite. Brian R. was still in high school. I was a year or two out of college.

Kevin joined the band in summer 1993; he was a friend of Brian R and a junior or senior year in high school. I liked them both right away. Brian R. was quiet and reserved. Kevin, not so much. When I started my record store in 1995, Brian R. and Kevin were my natural choices for employees.

Brian R.'s mother had owned a small business before. She graciously piled me with advice and information. She told me how to get my phone and electricity turned on and gave me the name of a good insurance company. These were things I had not thought much about. She also let me crash in a spare room for a few nights until I found a place. She has always been a sweet, supporting woman. Brian R. is very lucky. She also used to let every band in town practice in her garage. Her tolerance is saintly.

I met Brian R. while he was biting away at a hunk of Velveeta cheese like an apple. He is now a full-grown man, a husband, and a father, but I still picture him as a cheese-eating teenager in his mom's garage. He laughs when I bring the cheese up to him now.

I first saw Kevin when he was playing in another band. He was almost completely naked as he dove off the stage and landed headfirst on a metal folding chair, busting his mouth open. A couple of weeks later, I was introduced to him in Brian R.'s bedroom. I said, "Hey, I've seen you naked!" and Kevin looked a little embarrassed. He was maybe 16 years old. I was 24.

Kevin's mother is another dear woman. I still catch up with her now and then. She let me sleep on her floor and use her shower a number of times. For my first Easter in town, she gave me a basket of candy. My favorite Kevin story came from his mother's mouth.

After a particularly insane incident with teenage Kevin involving drugs, a hooker, and a chest wound, I was debriefing Kevin's unbelievably patient, understanding mother and she told me the tale of the first time young Kevin was left alone with a babysitter. The unequipped sitter took her eyes off baby Kevin for just a moment and he disappeared. The panicked sitter searched the house. He was nowhere inside. The sitter looked out a window to see baby Kevin, stripped of his diaper, perched high in the branches of a tree! I think this incident set a template for much of Kevin's future behavior: Nudity and danger.

Brian R. and Kevin worked the first several months of the record store, maybe even the first full year; I'm not sure. They left because they needed more hours than I could afford. I remember them being with me when I found the location and being by my side when I signed the lease. The day the store closed in 2008, Kevin gave me the nicest hug of the day and told me I did a good job. That made me cry.

They were also present when a representative from a credit card processing company set me up to take plastic. As he began explaining how to run credit cards and keep sales records, Brian R. and Kevin zoned out. They looked at each other and without a word—as if telepathically—got up, walked out of the retail space and into the storage area to play darts. They were so tight then, I think they could read each other's mind. The credit card guy said to me, "I guess you can explain it to them later."

My favorite Brian R. moment is from the second time the band toured in the summer of 1994. Brian R. had just finished high school. We were in New England, somewhere around Connecticut, very late at night. I was driving; it was Brian R.'s job to keep me awake. He had a sling shot and was shooting at signs and trees on the side of the road. Between shots, we spoke. I asked Brian R. what he would like to do with his life now that he had finished high school.

"I think I'd like to be an engineer," he said. This was a side of Brian R. I had never seen, rather serious-minded. I was impressed.

"Oh," I asked, "What kind of engineer?"

Brian R. paused, weighed the question and said, "The kind that drives a train!" As if there was any other kind. I chuckled over this at the time, but Brian R. was completely sincere. The one time I reminded him of it, he smiled.

That band lasted until August 1996. In October 1997, I started another band, Murder-Suicide Pact. I wanted to play with all new people, but at some point, Kevin seemed like the right guy for the job. I made a phone call and he was in for the next twelve years.

In 1999, a member quit and it seemed like the band was over. I called Brian R. to see if he would learn ten songs so I could play a set on my thirtieth birthday. He agreed to ten songs and one show. But somehow he remained in the band for fourteen years, three records, and I don't know how many concerts. Kevin, Brian R., and I playing music together again felt good. Brian R. is a professional and I can always count on him to be punctual, prepared, and precise. Kevin is a wild man. We could always count on him to provide excitement.

Kevin left the band in 2010. We don't see each other as often as I'd like, but when we do, he is warm and funny. I feel a deep affinity for him. I hope he feels it, too.

My relationship with Brian R. has become strained for several years. Aside from our band, I don't think we have much common ground. To be fair, he was a teen when we met in 1993 and is a grown man with a family now.

There are times when Brian R. gets on my nerves and I'm sure he feels the same way about me. When we toured the U.K. in 2008, he was so rude to me that I wanted to punch him at least twice, but I restrained myself. I wanted to finish the tour and keep the band going. If I punched him, it would have been the end of the music. At the time, playing music meant everything to me. Now I know there are more important things.

Kevin and the crowd at Sound Idea, Oct. 1999.
Photographer unknown.

WHO: ELLA

In late February 1995, I moved across the state of Florida, from Stuart on the Atlantic coast to Brandon, a suburb of Tampa, to open a record store. The Tampa area had a lively music scene and I wanted to be part of it. Brandon seemed like a great place for a record store, with so many young people and active bands. I had been a regular visitor to the vicinity for a few years and made a handful of friends, but basically, I was diving into unknown waters.

I had an appointment with a real estate guy to look at a storefront on the corner of Kings Avenue and Oakfield in Brandon, but the guy stood me up. So, I went exploring the town on my own, looking for vacancies. A red and white "For Rent" sign on the corner of State Road 60 and Parsons caught my eye.

The strip mall had a western look, with rickety, plank sidewalks and chunky, wooden square support beams holding up a wooden shingle awning over the walkway. The storefront was long and narrow. The whole place kind of looked like a ranch. I liked it.

The rent was a little out of my price range, but I had enough money in the bank to make a gutsy gambit. I offered the landlord half the rent he was asking and told him I would pay cash in full right then for an entire year. I was not sure he'd go for it, but I had nothing to lose by asking. It got his attention. It was much less money, but he'd get a huge wad of cash all at once and not have to worry about this cocky asshole for a full year. I figured the guy would pocket the cash and keep it off the books.

After mulling it over for a day and a half, the landlord called me back with a counter offer: Seventy percent of his original asking price, paid month-to-month on a one year lease. It was still a good deal, so I took it. I stayed in that spot for a little shy of fourteen years. My rent went up every couple of years, but by the time I went out of business, I still was not paying his 1995 asking price. I attribute part of the store's longevity to that crazy offer I made on the day I found the place.

I moved in and with the help of Brian R. and Kevin and we whipped the place into shape in a matter of weeks. For several days, I was constantly driving a couple of miles west on State Road 60 to a national chain hardware store for supplies. One day, one of the guys asked me, "Why don't you use the hardware store across the street?" I didn't know there was a hardware store across the street. I never noticed it, but there it was: Brandon Supply, one of the oldest businesses in town.

As I went to check out, I noticed the cashier was a stunning woman, maybe a few years younger than me. Most striking were her huge, intense, blue eyes. I was captivated. She rang up my purchase and smiled her lovely, sincere smile. Her voice was friendly, clear, and warm. I blushed a little. I walked across the street in an elated daze, wondering why such a beautiful woman was working at a gritty hardware store.

Back at the record shop, Kevin and Brian R. were working on something and Rob was hanging out, watching the progress. I was still glowing from seeing such a riveting woman. I excitedly told the guys about her and asked if they noticed her.

"You mean the one with the crazy, blue eyes?" Brian R. asked.

"Yes," I said, "But they're not crazy, they're beautiful. I'm going to ask her out."

"Good luck," said Rob. They all laughed.

I didn't have a good track record with pretty girls. But this was a new town. Nobody knew me yet. That pretty girl at the hardware store didn't know anything about me. I had a chance. I walked back with the intention of getting thumbtacks, an air conditioning filter, and a date.

When I entered Brandon Supply, I noticed the pretty girl was not at the cash register. I hoped she hadn't gone home for the day. Just as I was worrying that I'd missed her, she walked straight up to me and asked if I needed help. (I can still see her in her denim overalls.) I asked her to help me find the thumbtacks and the air conditioning filter. She took me right to them. (And I still have that pack of red thumbtacks. I never used them.)

"Is there anything else?" she asked. She was smiling.

"Yes, would you like to go out with me?" I looked down at my shoes, a little embarrassed and expecting a no.

"Yes." Still smiling, now broader, more beautiful. Shining.

She answered without the slightest hesitation, as if I'd asked her the time. I didn't even know her name. Ella. To this day I consider asking her out the greatest decision I've ever made. Months later, I asked her why she said yes. She said she thought I was cute and that I seemed harmless. She said she liked my shoes and that she checked out my ass the first time I was in the store.

We picked an evening, the soonest one we coud agree on. Our first date was at a Mexican restaurant. I had not been on a date in a while and never with a woman as attractive as Ella. I was talking too much, too loud, and too fast. I felt like I was out of control. I kept telling myself to calm down and to not fuck this up.

Ella could sense my nervousness. Just before our dinner came, she winked at me with her right eye. It was funny and sexy and flirty all at once. It seemed to say, "Relax, I like you. And after dinner you'll get to kiss me." This wink is my favorite memory in the world. I have replayed it hundreds of times. I wish I could return to that second.

We had more dates. I fell in love with Ella fast and hard. One night when we were sitting somewhere, I told her that I loved her. This took her by surprise. She hesitated but responded, "I love you, too." She didn't mean it. Not yet. I could tell. It was OK.

I don't know exactly when Ella fell in love with me, but I can tell you when I'm sure she was there. I was renting a bedroom from a family in Brandon. They had a swimming pool. Ella spent the night in my room many times; one night we decided to go swimming. I gave her one of my T-shirts to wear.

In the pool I cradled her in my arms and twirled her around in the water. It was like ballroom dancing. Her hair was wet. She was smiling her perfect smile. Her eyes gleamed better than the stars. We looked at each other and I just knew it. That was when I was sure she loved me back.

We stayed together for a very long time. Seven years after our first date, almost to the exact day, we were married. People asked us why we waited so long. The time just flew by. We didn't think that getting married would make us love each other more, so it didn't seem that important. You hear people say that all the time. But when we finally did get married, I do think I loved her more. It made me feel closer to her. I consider marrying Ella my greatest accomplishment.

BLACK FLAG
JEALOUS AGAIN 12"
SST RECORDS 1980

Black Flag's barrage of hard-hitting vinyl coupled with their relentless tour campaign made them punk rock royalty and living legends. Like many tens of thousands of malcontents all over the world, their terse lyrics and disjointed noise struck a nerve with me.

Black Flag had a constantly changing roster. The endless work schedule and pressure of being in the most intense band in the world burned members out. They had four vocalists during their original lifespan, 1978-1986. The second singer was Chavo. *Jealous Again* is not my favorite Black Flag record, but it is the one that Chavo sings on and I have a Chavo story—I think.

When I opened my record store in 1995, one of the labels I was most excited to carry was SST Records, home of Black Flag, Descendents, Bad Brains, Hüsker Dü, and many other primordial greats. SST was built on direct-to-store sales and was the prime example for many independent labels and a major middle finger to the mainstream music business. For a few years I bought directly from SST.

For about a year, I had a most persistent sales rep at SST who would call me without fail every Friday. I did not need to order from SST every Friday but he called anyhow. So, one Friday the little badger called me to ask if I needed to make an order and on that particular Friday I did indeed. However I did not have time to put together a list just then. I promised I would call back on Monday with a juicy order. He said, "Great, have a nice weekend," and hung up.

On Monday I called to make my order and the guy was canned. In fact, the entire sales department was canned. I was told by someone on the phone that SST no longer dealt direct to stores and that I would have to buy SST product from my choice of three large distributors. An hour later I received a form letter fax stating what I was told over the phone: SST no longer had a sales department. My poor, oblivious sales rep had no idea that Friday was his last day!

I protested. I called SST and asked them to continue dealing direct with me. I asked them to reconsider the whole thing. It seemed incongruent with their history and ideals. I did not want to buy from a big distributor and pay a big mark up. SST was already the most expensive domestic label I carried and now I was being forced to go through a middleman and take a price increase. Under those circumstances, I could no longer afford to carry one of my favorite labels. I was put through to Chuck Dukowski, bassist of Black Flag and former co-owner of SST.

Guitarist Greg Ginn has been called the brain of Black Flag and Chuck Dukowski has been called its heart. I was in awe to be speaking to one of the founding members of Black Flag. After a bit of chit chat and after Dukowski fielded a few Black Flag trivia questions, we got down to brass tacks.

Dukowski reviewed my sales records for the last few years and flatly told me that in the last year I had not spent enough with SST for them to continue dealing direct to me. Chuck was impressed with my first year of sales, but noted a steady decline over the last couple of years. True, sales were not as good. I explained that if I could not order direct, I would not be able to afford to order at all. Even so, SST cut me off. When the last of my SST stock was gone, that was it for my shop.

Six months later, a guy and a woman walked into my record shop. The guy looked a lot like Chavo. He seemed the right age, right height, everything. He was intrigued by the décor: early American punk rock. He closely scrutinized the old show flyers on the walls with a look that said, "Well, I'll be darned." He glanced at me a couple of times to size me up, seeing if I knew anything about punk rock. Then the guy went directly to the "B" section of the CDs, flipped through a few rows, turned to his girlfriend and said, "A punk rock store with no Black Flag CDs. Let's go!"

To this day I am 99 percent sure it was him.

CULT RITUAL
S/T 7"
BURRITO RECORDS 2007

I'd known all of the guys in Cult Ritual since before they could drive. They all used to hang out at my record store, watching bands and talking about music. I made lots of tapes for them, stuff I figured they needed to know about. They were music hunters. They probably would have found it all without me, but I gave them a head start.

They were in other bands before Cult Ritual. All of these bands played at the record shop numerous times. I let some of these groups practice in the storage room on Sunday afternoons. That's how they met each other, hanging around the shop. I watched the four of them grow up, as people and as musicians. They were nice kids. Now they are nice young men.

The four had chemistry. They worked together in a way that couldn't be forced. It was the right combination at the right time. They were half my age and I envied them.

I missed the first Cult Ritual show. It was at a house party somewhere in the Tampa area. I didn't know where the place was and I didn't think it was a good idea for me to go to a party with a bunch of people 20 years younger than me. I was starting to feel an age gap about this time. So, I didn't go, but I heard it was great.

I wanted to see the band, so I asked them to play at the record store and they did. It was their second show; I was blown away. A band I was playing bass for played that night, too. I thought we were hot shit. Then Cult Ritual played and we fell short in comparison. I wondered if it was a fluke. Were they always that good? Weeks later, I saw them play for the second time and again they rocked hard. I strongly considered them for my record label. I wanted to grab them before someone else did, but I wanted to see them again, just to make sure.

I asked Cult Ritual to play a free show in front of the Brandon Regional Library on New Year's Day 2007. This was kind of a tradition in our area. Bands would play outside of the library on legal holidays, without permission, when the place was closed. There are numerous electrical outlets around the building. It is an odd setting for a concert, plus I like the concept of people expressing themselves with music in front of a repository of words and ideas.

Cult Ritual played to about three people but didn't hold back. Once again they overwhelmed me. After the show, I asked them if they'd like to release a record on my label. I got a quick yes. I'm glad I got in on the ground floor.

They had a home recording that they wanted to use. It was OK, but I knew we could do better. I told them I wanted to bring them to a good studio and make a record that would sound awesome always. The band was divided on this. A couple of them felt strongly about the home recording. Eventually, they agreed and I booked time with my own money at the best recording studio in town.

The session was on Mother's Day. This, too, was a minor issue, as they had to do things with their mothers. I told them the session would start in the afternoon so that they could spend the morning with their mothers. And that's what they did.

In a few hours, the band cut seven songs, enough for a solid EP. But the vocals seemed a little off. They were not as strong as they could be, so the singer took a rest and then re-recorded all of the songs. This time they were perfect. The next day he realized he had a throat infection. He recorded those songs with a raw, inflamed throat full of gross, white pus. (Maybe that's why he sounds so agitated.) And about a month later, the record came out.

I was happy with the record and so was the band. Since they were a new band and this was their first record, I did my best to promote them. I disliked this part of the record business. In the past, there were fewer records and less hype. If a good record came out, people would pick up on it naturally. Little promotion was necessary. But by the 2000s, there were so many labels in the game that aggressive publicity was essential for survival. I found this distasteful and tried to promote in an honest manner, free of hyperbole and gimmicks. This approach proved to be largely ineffective. The game had changed.

The record sold moderately. Overall, it tied as the second-worst-selling release on my label. Had I not gone out of business the next year, it probably would have done more. I thought the record was dynamite and should be selling much faster. But I didn't have any other tricks up my sleeve. I left it to the record buying populace to decide.

Even though I had sold only a couple hundred copies of the record, I wanted to follow it up. I asked the band if they'd let me put out another record. Unlike the first time, they deferred me. I asked again, maybe a week later, and one of them told me that they had offers for their next couple of records and that *maybe* I could do their *fourth* release. Maybe? Fourth? I was insulted. And who was giving them offers? Their only record had only sold a couple hundred copies. Hardly anyone had heard it.

So, the band did a few more records on other labels that sold well while I barely sold any of my release. As their newer records went on to be overnight Internet collectors' items, I was still sitting on hundreds of copies of the debut. I was only asking three dollars each for their first record, while their other titles were going for up to and more than one hundred dollars each on eBay. I thought the one I put out was their strongest effort. It didn't make sense. But, whatever.

The band spent a lot of time touring and I barely saw anything of them for the next year. I was glad that they were taking off in popularity, but I could not understand why that first record sold so slowly. I got a little pissy about the whole situation. To add insult to injury, when the band was interviewed in a big magazine, one of the members put down the record I released, saying it was their worst one. Another member chimed in that the studio engineer didn't know what he was doing. I felt betrayed and wrote them all off as dicks.

When I went out of business, I had 200 copies of the Cult Ritual record left. I sent these and some other dead stock to a distributor in California who promised to pay me one dollar each as they sold. The other Cult Ritual records were eBay gold, mine was dollar bin filler.

Cult Ritual was one of about eight bands to play my going-out-of-business party. By then, a lot of my sour feelings toward them had dissipated. And I think they became more grounded after their lofty year as an underground buzz band died down.

A couple of years after all this, one of them told me that he felt bad about the magazine interview and that he thought my release was their best output. I've become close to him. A long time ago, I decided that I never wanted to have children, so I had an operation. Not long ago, I started calling this one my son and he has let me.

Cult Ritual playing at 113-H's last night of business, Oct. 18, 2008. Photo by Kyle Stone.

DEAD BOYS
YOUNG, LOUD, AND SNOTTY LP
SIRE RECORDS 1977

The Dead Boys were late. Really late. A couple of hours had passed since the opening band. The audience was getting antsy and loud. There were rumors they'd canceled. The lobby of the club buzzed with talk of no refunds. There were rumors of a car crash involving the band.

The band started in Ohio in 1976 and soon moved to New York City, a smart career choice. By 1979, the Dead Boys were dead, leaving behind a pair of seminal studio albums and some large footprints. They have left a huge impact on punk rock around the world. They were on Sire Records, a subsidiary of Warner Brothers, sharing a roster with the Ramones and eventually Madonna.

I was too young to catch the Dead Boys in their first life, but in 1987 the band was resurrected with all five original members for a tour commemorating the tenth anniversary of their first album. My friends and I drove a couple hours south to Miami for their only Florida appearance. The tour started in Miami, an odd place for a band from New York to begin a tour. The Dead Boys had a rocky history with Miami. In 1978, they had an infamously difficult recording session at Criteria Studios, where they recorded their second album, which is oddly the same place Eric Clapton recorded, "Layla." They broke up shortly thereafter.

Anyhow, the Dead Boys were late. Before I left, my mom made me promise to be home by midnight. My parents were stricter than my friends' parents, the subject of humor at my expense. I told my mom that it would be impossible to be home by midnight. I told her the concert might end around midnight and then we'd have a two-hour drive home. She told me that I should leave early to be home by curfew. I told her I didn't think that would happen.

A car horn blew from the driveway. My friends always honked the horn, rarely came to the door. This was something my parents complained about. They probably wanted to avoid my parents, which was fine with me. My friends were weird and I didn't necessarily want my parents to see them, either.

"Midnight," my mother said sternly as I jogged for the door. I didn't answer.

I think it was just after midnight that the club made an announcement: "The Dead Boys are here and will be on soon." There was much cheering. I asked someone for the time. I was going to be pretty late but this was worth it. Right?

I called my mom from a pay phone and told her I was going to be really late. She told me to come home right then. I said I couldn't and hung up.

Another hour passed and the Dead Boys had not taken the stage. I started to get a little worried. I suggested to my friends that maybe we should leave. The idea was dismissed. OK, I was going to be really, really late. I hoped the Dead Boys would be really, really good because this might affect my concert-going future.

"Don't these Dead Boys know how late it is?" I wondered. It was well after one in the morning. Finally, the lights dimmed, the crowd roiled and a spotlight hit center stage. The Dead Boys at last.

Four figures walked on stage. The Dead Boys had five members. Even I knew that. I heard someone say, "No bass?" The bass player was missing.

Before the first song, singer Stiv Bators said they were normally a five piece but now they were a four piece. He said this with finality. Then he cryptically asked, "Do you know what it's like to see your best friend fly face first through a windshield?" And he left it at that. The audience assumed that bassist Jeff Magnum had been killed. (He hadn't, but I didn't find out until five years later.)

The band looked grim. Given the circumstances, could you blame them? They didn't look like they were having any fun on stage. A big, fat guy climbed on stage to dance. He ran halfway across the stage and tripped on something. He fell on his face. Stiv Bators stopped singing in mid-song, pointed at the guy and laughed a dark, mirthless laugh.

The band played four songs before guitarist Cheetah Chrome threw down his instrument and stormed off stage. The rest of the band looked at each other for a few seconds then followed him slowly with heads hung low.

The audience was confused. There were a few claps and a few boos. We were not really sure what we just saw.

Did the Dead Boys just break up before our eyes? Was Jeff Magnum really dead?

The crowd waited for a few moments until the house lights came up and recorded music came over the P.A. system. The show was over. A few people yelled, "Bullshit!" and "Refund!"

The crowd milled around in the lobby and on the sidewalk in front of the club. The air was tense. The talk was feverish. The box office was black. There would be no refunds.

Two of my friends and I stood on the sidewalk, waiting for another who'd disappeared in the post-concert confusion. From behind us came a jostling. People were being pushed or jumping out of the way of something. I looked over my left shoulder to see a very scary, bald man, shoving people out of the way. His scowl was dark and deep. It was Dead Boys guitarist Cheetah Chrome, still in his stage clothes, coming straight through the crowd like a bulldozer. A second after I caught a glimpse of his face, he thrust his right palm into my left shoulder, knocking me back into a few people.

Cheetah stomped off the sidewalk, straight into Washington Avenue without looking at traffic. A car came very close to hitting him. But he didn't flinch or slow down. He marched straight across the road into a liquor store and we never saw him come out. I got home about 5 A.M. It was totally worth it.

DEAD KENNEDYS
FRESH FRUIT FOR
ROTTING VEGETABLES LP
CHERRY RED 1980

The Dead Kennedys album *Fresh Fruit for Rotting Vegetables* was the first punk record that I ever bought. It was a real eye opener. That it has remained in my all-time top ten for decades is a true testament to this record's magic.

I was in high school in a small south Florida town. I'd been exposed to punk rock through a series of mix tapes, borrowed records, and crudely-printed publications with titles like *Tropical Depression, Don't Ask Me, Sick Teen, Flipside,* and *Maximum Rocknroll.* A kid at my high school even printed a magazine called *Hey Old Lady, Pull My Noodle.*

Cooler, older friends would let me borrow obscure records. I asked them where they obtained these treasures. The answers were always vague and somewhat romantic: "a store in New York while I was on vacation," an older brother in college"and, the most intriguing, "mail order."

Mail order? It seemed weird. You send a person you've never met some crumpled up dollar bills in an envelope and a month later, a record would appear in your mailbox. In the year to come, I would become a mail order expert, but at the time, I was a little leery of such a practice. Seemed like a good way to lose your money. A couple of times it was.

So, for the time being, I would borrow records and make tapes. Until my friend Chris Oliver discovered a record store 40 minutes north of our town that stocked punk records. It sounded too good to be true. We began making weekly trips there, every Friday, right after school.

The store was Record Bar, a chain store in Fort Pierce's Orange Blossom Mall. The manager was a cool guy named Scot Lade. Scot was not only a punk—he played bass in Foul Existence and Disorderly Conduct. To us small town kids, Foul X and D.C., as we called them, were as big as internationally-known acts like Black Flag and the Misfits. Plus we could talk to them and they talked back to us. Amazing.

Anyhow, Scot used his managerial position to stock Record Bar with stuff no place else carried, not even mom and pop stores.

On my first trip to Record Bar, I was determined to buy a Dead Kennedys record. I knew a few of their songs from all the mix tapes and borrowed records; they seemed to be the most talented, humorous, and strange.

Record Bar had a few rows of LPs that they called "the import section," even though many of the releases were domestic. "Import" was record shop jargon in those days for anything that wasn't mainstream. I couldn't believe that there was a place just a car ride away from my school that stocked all of this crazy stuff.

I picked up the Dead Kennedys album *A Skateboard Party* and approached the sales counter.

"So, you like the Dead Kennedys?" Scot asked. He wasn't mocking my decision. He was truly interested.

"Yeah," I said, "I like a lot of the songs on this album."

"Well," he told me, "That album is a bootleg live recording and it is not the best example of their work. Do you own *Fresh Fruit?*"

No, I told him, I did not.

"I highly suggest picking up *Fresh Fruit* first. It's a better place to start."

He was sincere. I respected his advice. He walked me back to the rack and picked out a fine copy of *Fresh Fruit* for me. I thanked him, made my purchase, and left with my friends.

On the way home, we stopped at a Wendy's restaurant and looked at our new records while we scarfed down fries and shakes.

Chris bought seven records, all kinds of stuff. He was a nut. Just absolutely crazy about music, any style as long as it rocked him. I could never understand his penchant for Pink Floyd, but he loved them just as much as he loved Motörhead, the Butthole Surfers, George Clinton, and Run DMC. That guy was one of a kind.

Mike Maguire bought the *Punk and Disorderly* compilation album with Blitz, Partisans, Peter and the Test Tube Babies, and all those U.K. '82 stalwarts.

Jason got something by the Fall and/or Joy Division. That stuff was part of punk, too.

But everybody agreed that my copy of *Fresh Fruit* was the score of the day. The cover art was iconic. There was that giant, crazy, two-sided poster. And it was on blue vinyl, which none of us had ever seen. Whoa. This record blew us all away and we hadn't even played it yet!

Chris dropped me off at my house and then peeled out all over the neighbors' lawn as he drove away. Mike screamed something ridiculous and probably obscene, as he was wont to do in such cases. The neighbor ran out and started yelling. All I could do was say, "Sorry" before going inside and listening to the entire Dead Kennedys record four or five times.

I devoured the lyrics off the poster as Jello Biafra spat them out in his bizarre, sarcastic vocal style. The music was just as fantastic. It was hard to pick a favorite song—they all ruled! Within a week, I had every lyric and note etched into my long-term memory. To this day, I still burst into verses of "Stealing People's Mail" and "Chemical Warfare," for no reason at all, often at inappropriate moments, like weddings and bar mitzvahs.

Fresh Fruit continues to be somewhat of a measuring stick for me. Most records don't stack up to it and few surpass it. It is, for me, the essence of what punk rock is supposed to be: Interesting, humorous, thought provoking. Soon I started mowing lawns in my neighborhood, saving money for every record I could get my hands on. Just about every Friday, we made the trek to Record Bar, where Scot would play records for us and advise us on our purchases. I don't think he ever steered me wrong.

WHERE: PO BOX 3204

My permanent address since early 1995 has been PO Box 3204. This is the address I ran my record label and mail order company from. Later I ran my music merchandising company from there, too. Those companies are long gone, but I keep the box so people can always reach me.

PO Box 3204. I've rubber-stamped that address on tens of thousands of letters and parcels. Some of the staff at the Brandon Post Office have become like family to me. We've seen each other grow old. I can't guess how many thousands of hours I have spent in line and at the counter of that place.

At the counter is where I made friends with the clerks Laura, Gail, Dianne, Ed, and the rest. At the counter we talk about our personal lives: friends and family, vacation plans, food, illness, cars, and daily life. Laura helped me open the PO box in 1995. She's not there anymore. And Ed passed away a few years ago. I still see Gail and Dianne now and then. When Dianne is not on the counter, I can usually hear her laughing from back in the mail handling room. Gail is usually on the counter.

I brought Ella to the counter with me a few times. They all liked her. Everyone likes Ella. The day we got married, I worked half of the day to handle the mail order. That day, Ed was working the counter. He weighed and metered my packages and when he was about finished with the load, I told him I was off to get married. He broke a wide, sincere smile and shook my hand.

My permanent address. Photo by Bob Suren

DICTATORS

GO GIRL CRAZY! LP
EPIC RECORDS 1975

I was a ninth grader at Martin County High School in Stuart, sitting at one of the many mandatory-attendance pep rallies that our school administration thought was just as important as say, math or English. All the weird kids who clearly did not give a shit found each other and sat in one area, not cheering, looking bored, and talking about music. It was at one of these pep rallies that I first heard Motörhead on a boom box.

As the more spirited members of the student body screamed their lungs out for the fucking MCHS Tigers, we quietly discussed the Dead Kennedys, our hatred for jocks, and general angst.

Between cheers of "TIGERS!," during the three second lull between the crowd roars, someone sitting directly behind me shouted, "PAP SMEAR!!!" at a shattering volume and pitch directly into my right ear. It was so loud, it hurt. I wanted to punch whoever blasted my poor ear. I spun around to see a cackling 15 year-old Mike Maguire, clutching his gut and red with laughter, obviously delighted with his wit. Then it occurred to me exactly what he yelled and I started laughing, too. That's how I met Mike and although we have not lived near each other in decades, we have been friends ever since.

Mike dressed like a combination of punk icon Darby Crash and Mr. Furley from *Three's Company*. He called himself the Reverend Fucking Mike Anarchy, because all good punk rockers had a nickname. My mother hated him and probably still does. (He once got Chris Oliver and me arrested for an indiscretion with a BB gun and a Kentucky Fried Chicken sign.)

By eleventh grade, Mike and I shared a locker. One day I forgot my English book and ran to the locker in the middle of class to get it. When I opened the locker, two large bottles of liquor tumbled out, like something out of a movie. There was a school security guard in the hall. He heard the clatter and saw me stuffing something back into the locker. He was making his way over to me, so I took off running to class with my English book. Later in the day I told Mike to please get the alcohol out of our locker and he did (by drinking it, I assume).

Another day, almost the exact same thing happened with a Ziplock bag of magic mushrooms. Sharing a locker with Mike Maguire could be trying. However, sometimes it was rewarding. One day I opened the locker and found the first Dictators album, *Go Girl Crazy*.

Mike told me he didn't know who they were but the cover, featuring smiling singer Handsome Dick Manitoba clad in 1970s pro-wrestling attire, striking a cocksure pose in a men's locker room, was so stupid he had to buy it.

He let me borrow the album and it was, of course, sheer brilliance. Mike's copy of *Go Girl Crazy* made the rounds at MCHS, passing from weirdo to weirdo until we all had dubbed copies.

Eventually I found my own copy. And then another. And then another. I think I have owned at least a dozen copies of *Go Girl Crazy* over the years. Every time I see one, I pick it up if I can afford it and pass it on to someone who needs to hear it. (And if you have not heard it, it means you need to.) When my pal Frank Vagnozzi passed away in 2003, I was pleased to find two copies in his collection.

DISORDERLY CONDUCT
AMEN LP
DIRGE RECORDS 1986

This is one of a handful of records that my older sisters gave me for Christmas over the years. I received this for Christmas 1986, soon after it came out. Disorderly Conduct was from a bit north of the small south Florida town where I grew up. They were the local heroes; to a few of us, they were like gods. My friends and I saw them several times at all kinds of venues. DC headlined most of the local shows and frequently opened for touring acts that passed through Florida.

All of the guys in Disorderly Conduct were cool people and accomplished musicians, but the two who made the biggest impression on me were bassist Scot Lade and singer Casey Chaos.

Scot was probably the oldest guy in the band. At one time I heard him mention that he was 23 and I remember thinking how old that sounded. Scot was a great bassist, but more importantly, he was a great guy. I recently found him on the Internet and told him how cool he was, but he modestly shrugged it off.

As the manager of the chain record store in the mall, he worked to get as much great punk and hardcore music as he could into the area. Scot was generous with his time and his opinions. He was snarky at times but always a straight shooter. The music mattered to him and he wanted to expose people to the best stuff out there.

Scot grew to know our tastes and would suggest just the right thing for each person. Scot used to let us hang out in his office—a glorified closet—jammed with records, posters and magazines. Once when he left us in there unattended, we raided his address book for phone numbers of famous punk rockers like Kevin Seconds, Tesco Vee of the Meatmen, and Metal Mike Saunders of the Angry Samoans. I remember calling the number for Kevin Seconds and his mother, the famed Ma Seconds, answered the phone. She told me that Kevin was on tour, but she talked to me for a while. Scot seemed to know everyone and everything.

Scot risked his ass and wallet to put on all ages punk shows at rental halls in our area. Usually it was just one or two shows a year, but they were good shows and people would come from all over the state for them. This was way before the Internet, so it was all word of mouth and photocopied flyers getting the word out. At every gig there would be people from Miami, Tampa, Fort Lauderdale, Jacksonville, and even from far away Atlanta. There was less going on then, so when something happened, it was a big event and people would drive for hours. The first gig I ever went to was a Scot Lade gig, eight bands for three bucks in a fire hall.

At another of Scot's shows, five bands at the Sons of Italy Hall in Stuart, he got on the microphone before the first set and made an earnest plea to the audience to behave and not wreck the place, as punk rockers were wont to do at that time. A few seconds after Scot made his spiel, the first band started playing and the slam dancers kicked in hard. As the pit neared full frenzy, one of my idiot friends screamed, "Fucking anarchy!" and tossed the contents of a bag of powdered donuts into the air. Simultaneously, another of my idiot friends tossed the contents of a bag of charcoal into the air. The doughnuts and charcoal hit the dance floor and were pulverized into disgusting gray soot by dozens of pairs of combat boots. The floor was finely coated with gross debris all night long and it was Scot who had to clean it up at the end. Furthermore, a window got broken and someone spray painted the building. Scot lost his security deposit and was rightfully bitter. Scot promoted one more gig after this. The bathroom got destroyed that night and Scot threw in the towel.

Casey was the singer of Disorderly Conduct. He made the band go. He booked the shows, did a lot of promotion, and was the face and voice of the band. And what a voice! Listen to the wail at the beginning of the first song. Wow. Blood curdler, for sure.

Because Casey was a minor celebrity and because he was so fucking cool, I always assumed he was much older than me. Years later we reconnected and I was stunned to find out that he is two months younger than me. He made this amazing album when he was seventeen years old. That makes it even more amazing.

I've seen Disorderly Conduct many times. But the first time I talked to Casey was at a gig in Port Saint Lucie, Florida. He was playing pool with someone and totally exuded cool. I had just acquired the album and wanted to tell him how much

I liked it. I just walked up to him and started talking. More like gushing, to tell the truth, and Casey was totally cool.

"What's your name?" he asked. I told him, he smiled, and we shook hands. I wonder if he remembers this moment. It was important to me that he was cool. Over the years I have met a lot of my punk rock heroes; when they are cool, it makes their music mean so much more.

Disorderly Conduct was potent live—I still can't believe how professional they were—and Casey was a big part of the reason. His on stage persona is riveting. He commands attention. (These days he continues to astound in his band Amen).

Twelve years after shaking hands with Casey at the pool table, I was in my second or third year running my own record shop. I got a phone call from someone asking for directions from the airport. I gave the guy directions, but then stressed that my store sold only punk rock and I didn't want to disappoint him if he drove all the way out.

"I know that. That's what I want."

About an hour later, this totally punked-out dude walked in and I assumed it was the guy who called. We started talking and after a minute I realized it was Casey. He'd changed a lot in the passing years but the face and voice were the same. It was great catching up with him. And he spent a fortune. He just kept on adding records to his stack while my eyes popped out.

We stayed in touch and over the next couple of years he spent thousands of dollars with me, buying records through the mail. Casey is a true music fanatic. He loves all kinds of music and once he gets into a band, he needs it all.

The first time Casey placed a large order from me, he never got it. It seems that the mail truck got into an accident and burned up. Fortunately, the parcel was insured and I was able to replace his order. If the story seemed fishy to Casey, he never mentioned it.

Casey Chaos, April 2013 at Johnny Ramone's grave, Hollywood, CA. Photo by Bob Suren.

WHO: SAM AND PETE

Sam and Pete are brothers who worked at my record store. I never had a brother, only two sisters. I watched Sam and Pete's interactions with interest, the way Dian Fossey watched the apes. They could fling the poop. Sam and Pete, that is. I am not sure about the apes.

Pete is the younger brother, but he discovered the store first. Shortly after the place opened in 1995, I was hanging out with a customer about my age when we spotted three or four teenagers walking across the parking lot toward the store. "Great" I thought, "New customers." I needed them.

Just as I was thinking this, my friend said, "You have to watch out for these kids. They're trouble. They'll rob you blind." They did look a little shifty.

So that first time Pete and his buddies were in the shop, I watched them like a hawk. They were not trouble. They were just kids with funny haircuts. But to be safe, I watched them the next couple of times. No problems at all. I am not sure what information my friend was basing his theory on.

Actually Pete was trouble, but never for me. He had a bad temper and often got in hot water at school for acting out. I recall a story about him throwing something at a teacher and getting expelled. When Pete was good in school, his mom would reward him by bringing him to the record shop and letting him pick out something. That's how I met Mrs. W., a very patient, understanding woman.

One year around Christmas, Mrs. W. came in with Sam's wish list. There was an especially offensive title on the list. I didn't want to show it to her, but I figured I'd let her be the judge. I pulled the item from the shelf and handed it to her for her perusal. I watched her slowly evaluate the item before shaking her head and saying, "As a mother, I can't bring myself to buy this." Those were her exact words. I completely understood and re-shelved it at once. But I am getting a little ahead of myself.

Pete went home and told Sam that there was a record store a few miles away that sold only punk rock stuff and skateboards. "Bullshit," said Sam, "There is no store like that in Brandon."

A little while later, Sam walked in, froze three feet from the front door, threw his arms over his head and exclaimed, "This place is awesome!" He had a long, green Mohawk. He was wearing a dog collar around his neck. His voice had not changed yet; it was somewhere between Minnie Mouse and Pee Wee Herman. I automatically deemed him the most annoying person on earth and hoped I'd never see him again.

Funny how things work out. Sam and Pete became two of my best customers. And within a year, when I needed new help, Sam was the first person I thought of. I had the phone numbers and addresses for most of my best customers from a contest I held at the store. I dug through the contest forms until I found Sam's, called him and offered him a part time job. His hamster-like squeals seemed to say, "You had me at, 'Is this Sam?'"

If I had known about Sam's inability to do anything in a timely manner, I probably never would have called him. But I didn't know. And by the time I figured it out, it felt like I was stuck with that loveable goofball. Around this time, Sam finished high school and started college. Somehow I ended up typing almost all of his college papers. I think it was because I could not stand to watch him type so slowly.

Also around this time, Pete started working at the shop. Pete was a great worker when he could get to the shop, but the thing is, Pete never learned how to drive. He couldn't come to work until he found a ride each day. Sometimes it took him so long to find a ride, that by the time he got to work, there was nothing left for him to do. Pete is now in his thirties and has something like three master's degrees—but a driver's license? Nope.

I remember one time Sam and Pete got into a fight in the parking lot. It was basically a bunch of name-calling and wild swings. Sam broke one of his fingers on Pete's head and didn't get it set. It healed crooked, like an old witch's finger.

Sam and Pete definitely have their share of quirks, which, at times, frustrated me to the point of lunacy. But we also slogged through an unbelievable amount of work together. The hours were often long, the pay always meager. At times we toiled against odds that defied logic. I remember one time the whole crew stayed up until dawn hand assembling thousands of records until we were delirious and half blind. I took everyone to breakfast at Waffle House when we finally finished.

Somehow, we got through it all. I am still amazed at some of the feats we pulled off in that tiny, suburban record store. But it was so much more than a record store. It was a lighthouse for every oddball in the area. It was a meeting place for like minds. It was a second home for misfits. It was a concert space and a rehearsal spot for bands. It was where many people got their first taste of live music. For others, it was the first place they performed publicly. It was where people hung out and made friends. I can't imagine doing all that with any other crew.

When I closed the shop in 2008, Mrs. W. gave me a nice card telling me that I was a success and thanking me for helping to raise her sons.

Pete working as the doorman at a Saturday night gig at Sound Idea. Photographer unknown.

D.O.A.
HARDCORE '81 LP
FRIENDS RECORDS 1981

The first D.O.A. song I heard was "The Prisoner" from their *Hardcore '81* LP. It was on a potent mix tape that included, among others, the Clash, Really Red, Dead Kennedys, Crass, Gonads, Feederz, Iggy Pop, the Conservatives and many more. I am glad that cassette somehow found me.

Anyhow, "The Prisoner" is pretty much D.O.A.'s calling card. It is as close to a "hit" as that band will ever have. Excellent song. So, when I began record buying, D.O.A. was on my short list of "gotta get anything I see." I picked up just about every D.O.A. record I could find, including bootlegs, but this is the one that I still play heavily. When I feel like listening to D.O.A., I spin *Hardcore '81* all the way through twice.

Hardcore '81 was a staple on the shop stereo. The brothers, Sam and Pete, were just as nutty about D.O.A. as I was. We all had our favorite songs, but we gravitated toward this album. One day we were sitting around talking about D.O.A.'s general excellence and came up with the idea of doing a tribute band.

We started with a list of about 30 songs and eventually narrowed it down to a more realistic thirteen. Pete would be our Joey Shithead, playing guitar and singing. Sam would be our Randy Rampage on the bass. And I was to play the part of punk rock drum god Chuck Biscuits. As we discovered, it was a tough act to follow. Or imitate, I guess.

One day when Joey Shithead called to sell records to the shop, I mentioned that we were starting a tribute band. He was humbly delighted. Through a series of phone calls and emails, Joey clarified a few lyrics we couldn't figure out and I think he might have given us the chords to at least one song. But the coolest part was when he sent me a bunch of D.O.A. promo photos so we could get the right look for the band!

We only practiced a few times, because band practice with the brothers was never easy- sibling bickering. There was lots of name calling—particularly, "dickhead"—and arguing about how to play the songs. Brothers.

We dubbed our tribute band Fucked up Baby, after the D.O.A, song, naturally. We included that number in our set as well as "Nazi Training Camp," "My Old Man's A Bum," "I Don't Give a Shit," "Race Riot," "The Ballad of Kenny Blister," "Tits on the Beach," "Disco Sucks"—"The Prisoner," of course—and a few more. Pete insisted on making real belches for the song, "I Don't Give a Shit," which made practicing it more than once or twice in a row very difficult.

Pete expertly mimicked Joey's trademark side-to-side head bobbing while Sam did his best to be the maniac that is Randy Rampage. And I gained enormous respect for Chuck Biscuits. Some of the songs I just could never do right.

We had "Woke up Screaming" on our set list but we cut it before the show because it just was not coming together for us. I asked Joey about that. He told me that while it is a slow song, it is a hard one to play. The secret, he told me, was not to rush it, find the groove. We never found the right groove.

Show day came and we got into wardrobe secretly as not to spoil the surprise. We were decked out in our best flannel, bandanas, and jeans. Sam wore my old motorcycle boots. I donned a bushy blond wig. We looked great and we sounded pretty good, too. Unfortunately, there is only one photo from this night and I do not have a copy.

A week or so after the show, I spoke to Joey on the phone, told him it went well and mailed him a copy of the flyer. Joey thanked me and said it looked really cool. I haven't spoken to him in years, but I hope he held onto it.

DRILLS
CERTIFICATE OF PENETRATION LP
BALLS OF STEEL RECORDS 1987

I sleep with a box fan on every night. The fan drowns out the constant ringing in my ears. I have tinnitus. I blame the Drills.

For a few exciting years, the Drills were a mainstay of Miami's underground music scene. They opened for many of the big, touring acts, usually blowing the headliners off the stage. I saw them a few times on their home turf, the Cameo Theatre. At the Cameo, the Drills were unbeatable. The first time I saw the Drills significantly damaged my hearing.

The Drills played second that night. For the first band, my friends and I hung back. But the Drills were tall, lean, and serious. They looked good and sounded like a freight train. It was obvious they were not fucking around. After a song or two, the furious Drills were so difficult to ignore that we pushed to the front and stood way too close to the Cameo's screaming-loud P.A. speakers.

The headliner that night was the big draw, but their set was truncated and unremarkable. We drove back from the gig talking mostly about the Drills. We had to talk loudly; our ears had been blasted. By the time I rolled into bed, my ears pulsed with a low, warbling sound. I had my ears blasted before, but not like this. I figured if I could just fall asleep, the warbling would be gone in the morning. It wasn't.

The low, warbling sound lasted for almost two days. I got worried. I thought I was going deaf. I thought I really fucked up. Should I tell my parents? Go to a doctor? Ignore it? When the pulsating surf in my ears subsided, it was replaced by a high-pitched ring. That was in 1986. My ears are still ringing.

I never wore ear protection to gigs. I don't think anybody did in the 1980s. The first time I saw someone wearing earplugs to a concert was around 1990; I thought he was a lightweight. I continued going to concerts without ear protection. The ringing got worse.

In 1993, someone convinced me to try earplugs. It made a difference. I had already done irrevocable damage to my hearing, but wearing the plugs would prevent it from getting worse. Since then, I have worn earplugs to every concert I've been to. I even wear them when I am working with loud machines.

Unfortunately, I have never been able to wear earplugs when I play music. I could never hear my playing correctly. So, my hearing continued to deteriorate with each band practice and concert I played. I often find myself leaning in to converse and asking people to repeat what they've said. This makes me the butt of jokes with my younger friends. I tell them that tinnitus is no joke and to wear earplugs. They don't and probably won't until it is too late.

In 2005, I was the road manager for a two-band tour. Alex Hood, the guitarist from the Drills, was playing in one of these bands. I liked Alex. We talked a lot. I told him how great the Drills were and all the times I saw them play. I told him how I copied the Drills album many times for many friends. Alex told me inside stories about the band. It was cool to shoot the shit with this veteran rocker.

One morning over breakfast at a hotel, I told Alex about how I thought the Drills ruined my hearing. Alex remembered the show. When I was done talking, he shrugged with indifference as if to say, "That's part of the job" and resumed eating his eggs without a word. It wasn't the reaction I was expecting. I don't know what I was expecting, but that was the end of that conversation.

Alex was usually open and friendly, but when the opening act was late one night and the concert was delayed for almost two hours, he got angry. When they finally showed up, they were unprepared and unorganized. As a professional, Alex was livid.

"What do you say we take these fuckheads outside and teach them a lesson?"

He was serious. It was really shitty that the band was so ill equipped but I don't think a street fight would have changed anything. I told Alex to calm down and everything would work out fine. I'm glad I never got Alex mad.

On February 4, 2013, I was out for a walk when my cell phone rang. A mutual friend called to tell me that Alex died after a long illness. Alex is gone but my ears are still ringing.

EAT
COMMUNIST RADIO/CATHOLIC LOVE 7"
GIGGLING HILTER 1979

Got it for free, sold it for a thousand. Nice work if you can get it. I could have asked a little more, but I sold it to a friend.

Communist Radio is one of the most sought-after punk records in the world. At one time, I had two copies.

The band made 500 copies, and, as the story goes, they tossed out about a hundred at the record release gig back in 1979. Many of these were destroyed by the crowd, making the record even more impossible to find. Legends like these drive up prices and keep record collectors awake at night. I know, I was one.

Communist Radio is one of my favorite records. For years it was one of the crown jewels of my collection. Yet by the time I sold it, I just didn't care.

F

YOU ARE AN E.P. 12"
INTENDO DISTORTO RECORDS 1984

"Your idiot friends are here!" Thanks, dad. My father especially hated my punk rock friends. He liked my friend who played sports and planned to go to law school. I haven't seen that friend since his wedding—a couple of decades ago.

I'd been into punk rock for a couple of years and it was time for my first show. Maybe two weeks earlier Dave Rat handed me a flyer for the show. He told me not to let any jocks or rednecks see it.

"MUSIC FOR THE NEW YOUTH!" the flyer screamed in bold letters. Sounds cliché, but that's what it was. A lot of our punk rock lives centered around beer and skateboarding and vague politics, but there was always an underlying feeling that we were part of something important. The new youth.

It was the first flyer I'd ever seen and it is still my favorite. I held onto it for 27 years before I passed it down to one of my best friends. Some of the bands on the flyer canceled but others jumped onto the show. It ended up being eight bands for three bucks in a small rental hall.

It meant something that Dave Rat handed that flyer to me, too. He was the number one punk rocker in our town and co-promoter of the gig. Dave wanted me there and that meant I was OK with him. To Dave punk rock was a cause; he welcomed new recruits.

As I made a break for the front door, my dad informed me that my jackass friend's car was dragging its muffler and that we should tie it up. We tied it up with a t-shirt. We could smell the shirt burning all the way to the show.

We pulled into the parking lot and it was full of weirdos. Shows back then were fewer, especially in our area, so when they did happen, it was a big occasion. People dressed up. It always amazed me that people would drive from across the state to see a few local bands in a rental hall. This was 1985, way before the Internet Age, so publicity was all word of mouth and eight-and-a-half by eleven inch photocopies. I loved all of those old flyers. I had my bedroom walls covered in glorious black and white cut-n-paste.

A couple of cops were already at the show. Cops appeared at almost every show and it almost always meant the show was over. It was never a question of, "What if the cops show up?" It was more like, "When will the cops show up?" You could practically guarantee a visit. (As a singer, I had cops take the microphone from my hand a few times.) These cops just sat there watching the parking lot, waiting for someone to fuck up, like a couple of fat vultures in green uniforms.

I noticed a few guys from my wood shop class. One of them was wearing an American flag like a kilt. He'd decorated the flag in black marker with the names and logos of his favorite bands. Someone ripped the flag from around his waist and the two of them began a tug of war. The cops didn't like that and made their move.

They told the punks to stop and tried to grab the flag. The punks told the cops that it was a free country and they could do whatever the hell they wanted. For whatever reason, the cops backed off. I still can't believe that happened. The cops just went back to sit in their car. That was the last cop problem of the night. Miraculous.

The show started; we all filed in and paid our three bucks to Scot and his girlfriend Dawn, who were working the door. They made people wearing spikes take them off so nobody would get hurt. The punks put their spikes in small, brown paper bags and wrote their names on the bags with marker. Dawn stored the bags under a table to be reclaimed after the show.

Since I had never been to a show before, I'd never seen slam dancing. It looked chaotic and like a lot of fun. I dove right in without understanding the etiquette of the pit. It looked like you could just do whatever the hell you wanted, but there were actually boundaries.

I'd been taking martial arts lessons for eight or nine years at this point. I'd just received my first-degree black belt. I thought the dance floor would be a great place to try out my spin kicks, jump kicks, leg sweeps, and rolls. This did not go over well. I got a lot of dirty looks and a couple of guys crushed me against a wall. I must have looked like an idiot.

Between bands, my friend Mike was in the hall getting a drink of water. He overheard a gang of guys talking about beating my ass. Mike started laughing and said to them, "You can't beat his ass! He's a black belt!" I was a black belt, but I don't think I could have taken on five or six full-grown men. The guys heeded Mike's warning and nothing happened to me.

It was the second miracle of the evening. I didn't know about any of this until the ride home.

All of the bands were good, but the one people seemed most excited to see was F, who played second to last. They did "Beating around the Bush" by AC/DC and "Clock Strikes Ten" by Cheap Trick, a couple of my pre-punk favorites. I thought it was cool that they had the same background as me. After they finished, I grabbed the set list; I held onto it for ages but eventually threw it away.

Nat King Kong from Ft. Myers was one of the replacement bands to jump on the show. They played last and invited people to get on stage to do whatever. I was standing right up front watching when someone handed a bass to me. I'd never held an instrument before, but I knocked out a few clumsy notes before passing it on to someone else. It was a spontaneous mess but a lot of fun. A scary looking skinhead girl with a small tuft of blue hair climbed on stage and beat a metal folding chair with a two-by-four. That was her contribution to the mess.

After the show, Mike said he wanted to buy a record from F. They were the only band on the bill with a record out at the time. We walked over to where they were selling their records and T-shirts. Records were five dollars; t-shirts were six, ironically. I thought it was funny that the shirts were more expensive than the record. (That record sells for a lot more than five dollars these days.)

We drove home, speaking excitedly about all of the great music and crazy people we saw. When we pulled into my driveway, Mike told me I could borrow the record for a while. I went into my room and even though it was late, I listened to the record a few times on headphones. The rush from that first show was potent. I had to be in a band.

Months later, my friend who played sports and planned to go to law school, the one my father liked, invited me to go see U2. In 1985, U2 was still kind of cool. They came from the underground. A friend in the UK saw them open for Discharge in 1980.

In 1985 a U2 concert was seventeen dollars. I'd just seen eight bands for three dollars. I went to the U2 concert and they played well, played the songs I knew, but it just was not the same. My friend who played sports and planned to go to law school thought it was the greatest thing ever. But it could in no way touch the primal, tribal, sweaty three-dollar gig in the rental hall.

Flyer handed to me by David Anderson.
Flyer by Jason Emmett.

F
FOUR FROM '84 7"
BURRITO RECORDS 2007

There were two bands from Florida called F. Over the years, this caused quite a bit of confusion and some bad blood among the members. Actually, one of the bands is still around.

The original F was formed in 1982 by singer Angelo Pillitteri, who goes by the stage name Flash. They are still active. With the exception of a few short breaks, Flash has keep rocking under the F moniker for decades and still puts on a jaw-dropping performance every time. Flash is about 55 now and he rocks harder than most teenagers. I have no doubt he'll be wowing audiences a decade from now. He is Florida's Iggy Pop.

Flash's version of F has been a revolving door of members. Around 1983, Flash had a dispute with the band's second guitarist about the way certain songs should be played. Depending on who you ask, Flash fired the guitarist, or he quit.

The guitarist felt that he had contributed heavily to a number of songs and that they were his. He took these songs and started a new band. If it ended there, things might not have become so nasty and twisted. But he took the band name with him, too. This is still a sore point.

The second version of F, the one with the fired guitarist, went on to become well known outside of the state. They put out a few records (that included the disputed songs), appeared on some compilations and toured the U.S. as the opening act for a popular band. A few years later, they broke up. Their records are sought after by collectors and very expensive.

In the meantime, and to much less acclaim, Flash kept his version of F rolling, playing mostly on the south Florida bar circuit. Flash's F made a few cassettes and later a few computer-made CDs, but no vinyl records. In the punk music scene, vinyl is credibility.

As a result of their records and touring, the second version of F is the one that I and many other people heard of first. In fact, many people have never heard of Flash's F at all. Around 1985, one of my friends found a cassette called, *The*

Danger Is Here! released by Flash's F. The sound, especially the vocal style, is very different. There were a few songs we already knew from the second F. We were confused.

Our information about music came from magazines and by word of mouth. Sometimes by the time info got to us, it was generations old and distorted. You can imagine how mangled the F story was by the time it got to us.

In 2003, I was the road manager for the Pork Dukes, a British band. We pulled into the club in Miami and I was shocked to see F listed as the opening act. I heard rumblings that Flash was still playing as F, but I had never seen them. A year earlier I had a chance in Tampa, but I skipped the show, arrogantly assuming it would be no good. That was a mistake, because when Flash and the 2003 version of F hit the stage that night in Miami, they blew the cobwebs out of my jaded brain.

They played the songs I was familiar with from the second F's records but also many others I had never heard. Flash jumped around like a man possessed, diving off the stage in several fits of abandon. During the song, "Smash It," he smashed a mirror with a hammer, spraying the audience with shards of glass. The band was tight. Flash put on an incredible show.

After their set, I talked to Flash for the first time. I bought two CDs, including *The Danger Is Here!* But most importantly, Flash wearily filled me in on the history of the two bands named F. He told me about the disputed songs. He told me of the guitarist who quit or got fired, and about another member who left him to play with the second F. The pieces of this weird puzzle fell into place. I tried to put myself into Flash's shoes and understand his frustration. Why did he keep playing all of these years? How did he maintain motivation?

F was the topic of discussion that night as we drove north in the tour van. The British guys liked the band, especially Flash. Like him or not, he's hard to forget. But most people do like Flash. When the Pork Dukes returned for another tour in 2005, they wanted F as the opening act every night. We made it happen.

I talked to Flash a lot on that tour. The more I talked to him, the more I liked him. His humor is quick. And watching him give so much of himself to music filled me with reverence.

The singer of the second F was at the show in West Palm Beach. He told me that he loved the original F and feels bad about the way things turned out. He told me how much he respects Flash and how excited he was for the concert. He was up front the whole night, cheering and singing along. It was odd watching the two singers of F share the microphone. I tried to figure out what Flash was feeling but I could not quite put my finger on it.

That night I asked Flash how it happened that the original F never made a vinyl record. He considered this for a moment. I am not sure it ever occurred to him. After a pause, he explained that he always financed the band. Money from shows was never enough to keep it going. He paid for band expenses out of his own pocket. And while the band recorded many times since 1982, a vinyl record was never within his means. The band made do with cassettes and later burned CDs in short press runs.

I stayed in touch with Flash. I was also in touch with the guitarist who started the second F. In 2007, I had the idea to put all of the F music—from both versions of the band—on a double CD. I wanted to give each band a disc and space in the CD booklet to tell the complete F story. I thought it was a shame that the music was so good, yet so hard to obtain. I also thought that a complete F release might mend fences. There were many issues at stake. Ultimately, I could not bring the two camps together.

I really wanted to get some F music back in circulation. And I wanted to untangle the contorted F story for record collectors everywhere. I asked Flash if I could release four of the songs from *The Danger Is Here!* as a 7" record. He loved the idea.

I asked Flash to send me as many photos and as much memorabilia from that era of the band as he could find. Fortunately, Flash saved everything. He flooded my mailbox with a torrent of images including photos, handbills, news clippings, and more. I couldn't believe he kept all of this stuff. When I saw it all spread out on my desk, it became very clear how important the band is to him.

I explained to him that this record had to tell the unheard F story. As part of the packaging, I wanted to include an in-depth interview with Flash, leaving no stone unturned.

So, for a few weeks, Flash and I played email tag. I sent questions; he sent answers.

A couple of times, Flash lost his cool and his answers were less than diplomatic. I reminded him that this record was going to reach a lot of people. It was his chance to tell his side of the crazy F story. I encouraged him to take the high road. He took my advice and rewrote a few of his answers.

When the interview was complete, Flash turned the tables on me. He said he wanted to interview me! I think he was just curious about me and maybe even a little skeptical of my motives. I thought this was very funny and complied. Flash sent me a series of questions, asking me about my personal life, my experiences in music, my education, and more.

But the last question was the greatest: "Why do you want to put out this record?" I told him that beyond being a record collector, I considered myself a music historian and that his story had to be documented. I told him how much I respected him for keeping his band going all these years in the shadow of the second F. He accepted that.

Late in 2007, I released the record *Four From '84*. It was the first vinyl release by Flash's F. And it was the last release on my label.

Flash and me at Churchill's Pub in Miami, Feb. 2008.
Photo by Pete Watson.

FAILURE FACE
S/T 7"
BURRITO RECORDS 1993

I had been in a few bands before, but Failure Face was the first serious one. Our drummer, Rob Sexton, had been in an active band that put out lots of records, did long tours, and worked in real recording studios. My only recording experience until then had been some rough home recordings.

For our first few months, we floundered around until we found just the right combination of members. After three practices with this lineup, Rob said we were ready to record. I thought it seemed a little premature, but I trusted his opinion.

Rob heard good things about a new recording studio in Tampa called Audio Lab. He booked us for a Saturday afternoon in April 1993. Before heading to the studio, we had a quick, refresher practice and right before it was time to leave, we came up with a new song. With the new one, we had six songs to record, enough for a 7" EP.

We got to the studio a little before schedule. Ken Faulkenberry, the owner, helped us load in our gear. He told us that Greg would be recording us and that he should arrive, "any minute." So we sat and waited. And waited. And waited.

Hours passed. No Greg. Ken set up the studio for us and kept telling us that Greg should be there soon. We were getting bored and angry. There was some talk about packing up and going home. Ken kept apologizing for Greg.

And then in walked Greg Marchak, four and a half hours late. This is what we were waiting for? He didn't look like much: Grossly overweight, unshaven, and wearing rumpled clothing. And he smelled. He smelled like he pissed himself a few days earlier and never bothered to clean up.

Greg gave an understated, mumbled apology and then said, "OK, guys. What are we doing today?" We all sort of hated him at this point, but we also wanted to record, so we put on our friendly faces and got down to work. Once we started rolling, Greg was great to work with. He worked fast, got the right sounds and was very funny.

Greg had a heavy New York accent and a brusque manner. He didn't bother to learn our names so he said things like, "Mr. Bass Player, will you please stop fucking up?" and

"Yo, moron, you missed your part." But it was funny the way he said it, not mean. He was like an insult comic. The Don Rickles of recording engineers. His catch phrase was, "When I say, 'rolling', we are indeed rolling. *Rolling!*"

The guys recorded their music first and then it was my turn to do the vocals. I was singing too hard and running out of wind. Greg taught me how to sing without losing my breath. And after that, everything came together. We had everything finished in just three hours. Six songs, recorded, mixed and mastered. The total cost was one hundred and forty five dollars. I've never recorded that quickly or cheaply again. We left the studio in good spirits. And we all decided that Greg was fantastic. He could use a shower, but fantastic nonetheless.

I had no idea if what we recorded was good or not. Rob and I went back to his house and listened to a cassette of the new recording. After a few minutes, Rob said, "This is awesome." That made me beam. I honestly didn't know what to think before Rob spoke. He said we picked the right studio and that it was a good thing we waited around for Greg.

We were so happy with the recording that we returned to work with Greg two more times, in 1994 and 1996. I think our music holds up pretty well, thanks in large part to Greg's studio skills. I recorded in other bands with Greg in 1998, 2000, and 2006. Greg's hygiene and punctuality improved moderately. His humor got more outrageous. He was the only guy I would record with.

In 2007, I took a young band to Audio Lab to work with Greg. I knew he was the right guy to capture their sound. He brought out their best and like most people, they thought he was hilarious.

And that was the last time I saw him. A couple of months later, Greg was at the studio, working on a project, when he complained about a headache. He went home, climbed into bed and died in his sleep. He was 46.

The late Greg Marchak hard at work. Photographer unknown.

FLAMING MIDGET
MIDGET MELODIES: VERY SHORT SONGS FOR THE VERY SHORT 7"
BURRITO RECORDS 1991

In the summer of 1990, I started a band with three strangers. I had been in a couple of bands before, but always with old friends. The girl I was dating introduced me to a guy who wanted to be a singer. At first I thought, "This guy? No way!" But after we talked a while, I realized he was cool and we discussed the strategy for our new band.

He had a guitarist and drummer in mind but needed a bass player. I owned a bass but had never played one in a band. Owning one was good enough. I met the other guys at our first practice.

We were an odd lot. I was firmly entrenched in punk rock. The singer wanted to play punk, as well, but was also into industrial music and hip-hop. The guitarist said his favorite band was Jethro Tull. He wanted to play long, ponderous, pretentious prog-rock but it quickly became apparent that nobody else wanted to do that, so he gave up pretty easily. (He was the odd man out in our already-odd lot.) The drummer just wanted to play. He was a classic rock guy, but when we played some punk rock stuff for him, he ate it up.

What we had in common was an odd sense of humor. We bonded over bad jokes, particularly puns and obscure movie references. During one of the first practices, we decided on the name Flaming Midget. It was nonsense; it was perfect. It was that or Exploding Panties. I think we made the right call.

I had been taking guitar lessons and learned a little music theory—just enough that I was itching to try my hand at songwriting. I'd written plenty of lyrics before, but never tried writing music to fit lyrics. Although my music and lyrics were very simple, I found the process challenging and satisfying. To this day, my favorite part of being in a band is putting a good song together. I ended up writing a large percentage of the band's music and lyrics, which became a sore point with the guitarist. (Toward the end of our run, he began bringing ideas to practice.)

After a handful of practices, we arranged our first

concert. In our small town, there were very few opportunities for bands to play, so we made our own opportunities. We invited all of our friends and family to come see us play at a picnic pavilion on the water. We had no permit, no permission. It was punk rock. We just showed up, plugged in, and rocked. We had only eight songs, so we played them all twice. While we were into the second set, a cop car pulled up. The cop got out and watched us play the last few songs. My guess is he was either so bewildered or so amused that it did not occur to him to break up the illegal gathering. When we were packing up, the cop asked me what the name of the band was.

Six days after our first show, we played our second and final show. Somehow, we secured an actual club date at an actual rock club with two other bands. The show was remarkable only in location. Three punk rock bands playing in a real club was definitely unusual for the time and place. We were something of a novelty to the owner. I'd like to tell you that something wacky happened, but it didn't.

A week or two later, the four of us went off to four different colleges. I stayed in touch with the singer and a little bit with the drummer. The guitarist sort of drifted away and none of us ever heard from him again.

About a year after our farewell show, I was at college, sitting on my bunk, plunking out the old songs on my bass. I thought the songs were good and felt that it was a shame we never recorded them. I'd been collecting records for seven or eight years and thought it would be cool to have my own music on a record. Imagine what it would be like to hear your own sounds coming out of a stereo. The idea tickled me for weeks. I had to find out how to make a record.

I knew a guy in Gainesville who'd just started a record label. I think he had two records out at the time. I knew him, but we were not really friends. I just knew who he was. I cold called him, found his number in the phone book and just called. I asked him how to put out a record. He invited me over for a talk.

He was exceptionally gracious with his time and knowledge. He was excited that I was trying. He gave me phone numbers and addresses for record pressing plants and told me of his experiences with each. He gave me step-by-step instructions for putting out a record. It was not that hard. Just like the concert at the picnic pavilion, no permission was necessary. Turns out all you needed was the money to do it.

I did not have the money to do it. It was not an impossible sum, but I fell just a little short. I ran the idea by the singer and the drummer. They offered to make up the difference. I promised to pay them back eventually but they said that was not necessary. They wanted to be on a record, too. We'd lost touch with the guitarist and didn't care enough to find him. I said I could record the guitar parts myself. They were basically the same as the bass parts.

The singer said his friend Joel could record us. We picked out a recording date and I jumped on a bus back to my hometown.

I didn't know anything about recording, but Joel said he'd done plenty and knew exactly what to do. His recording device was an ancient reel-to-reel machine with a quarter inch tape. We checked it out at his house. It didn't even look like the thing would work, but he plugged it in and the reels started turning. We heard what sounded like a very old college mathematics lecture coming from the speaker. That's when I realized that Joel's father had been my seventh grade math teacher. (I hated that guy.)

"We can record over this," Joel said. But we needed a place to record.

I knew of an abandoned house in a quiet neighborhood. The last time I checked, the place still had electricity. I went back to the place, broke in through the back door with a screwdriver and flipped a light switch. There was still power. A few hours later, we rolled tape, recording right over the old college mathematics lecture.

We did almost everything in one take. We recorded drums, bass, and vocals together for most songs. Then I went back and overdubbed the guitar. It was a two-track recording. Somehow, Joel rigged the ancient reel-to-reel machine to a tape deck and we made a mix-down to cassette.

I took this cassette with me back to Gainesville, where I was attending the University of Florida. I found a recording studio in the phone book. The name seemed somewhat familiar. I called up and explained that I needed help mastering a home recording.

I showed up at Mirror Image Studios with my little tape and waited in the lobby for someone to help me. There in a glass case in the lobby, I saw a copy of the first record by

Roach Motel, Florida's first hardcore punk band. I did not have that record at the time and I wanted it. I'd never even seen a copy. Then I realized where I'd heard of Mirror Image Studios. Roach Motel, Hated Youth, and Sector 4—three of Florida's earliest and most significant hardcore bands—had recorded there. And now I was here with my little tape.

Somebody finally acknowledged me. My first question was, "Can I buy that Roach Motel record?" The guy laughed and said no. The guy was engineer Bob McPeek who had recorded the band.

Bob took me into the studio and I handed him the tape. I told him that we recorded it at home but we wanted to make it sound as good as possible so I could turn it into a record.

"OK," said Bob, "Let's have a listen." He put on the tape and the look on his face was priceless. It was as if I'd just cut an enormous fart that he was trying to ignore. But after a few seconds, a look of recognition and a thin smile came across his face that seemed to say, "Oh, I remember this kind of music. Punk rock, right?" The guy was a total class act.

"I think we can clean this up a little," he said with copious tact, "We'll start by getting it into stereo." We'd recorded so badly that the music was coming mostly out of one speaker.

Bob diddled around with his gear and after a while said, "There, that's much better." He made a copy on digital audio tape for the pressing plant and a backup copy on cassette for me. I thanked him, paid him and went home to plan the record.

I was so excited at the prospect of having my band on vinyl that I couldn't sleep. There was so much to think about. Cover art. Lyric sheet. Vinyl color. The labels. I had a lot of ideas.

I also needed a name for the record label. At the time, I did not consider running a record label. I didn't think I'd ever put out another record, but I knew that records are released by record labels and even if this was a one-off project, I needed a name. At band practice, we'd often count off our songs by saying, "Uno, dos, tres... burrito!" It was just one of our stupid inside jokes. Burrito Records seemed like a good name. I drew up the Burrito Records logo that night while sitting on the floor of my place.

A month later, the record was finished. Hearing it for the first time through my own stereo was one of the greatest thrills of my life in music. All of our hard work, now in a tangible, permanent format. It was something I could hand to someone and say, "Hey, this is my band."

The other guys were pleased, too, but not being record collectors, it did not seem to mean quite as much to them. A few local music people asked me how our band, "got a record deal". It was the same question I'd asked the band F several years earlier at my first concert. My answer was the same as theirs: There was no deal, we did it ourselves.

I sent off a few copies to magazines for review and waited. Months later I had not seen any reviews. What was the delay? Then one afternoon in a record store, I picked up a copy of *Maximum Rocknroll* and flipped to the review section. There it was! Our band name in bold type! My heart missed a beat. "This is awesome," I thought. Then I read the review.

It was a terrible review. More than terrible, it was mean. I was crushed. It was the first time I put something I created out for public criticism and I got pounded.

I went home and wrote a scathing letter to the reviewer. I specifically said that I did not want the letter published in the magazine. I just wanted the reviewer to read my letter and realize what a fucking dick he was. So, of course, the letter got published.

And I came across looking like kind of a crybaby. But, the letter had an unusual effect: People started ordering the record! Many of the orders I got for the record said things like, "This sounds like the kind of record I want to hear" and "If that guy hated it, I'll probably love it." It was not how I envisioned my entry into the record business.

A short time after that terrible review, I came home from work to find an envelope on my desk from the Alternative Tentacles record label. I opened it up and inside was a note from Jello Biafra, owner of Alternative Tentacles Records and singer of the Dead Kennedys, arguably one of the most important punk rock bands of all time.

Jello wrote that he'd been looking for my record since he read the review and he could not find it anywhere. He asked me to send him "five or ten" copies and in return he'd send me some stuff on his label. I was beyond stoked. The Dead Kennedys were one of my favorite bands. I wanted to be like

Jello. My worship of Biafra made me pick up the microphone in 1985. Hell, yeah.

But why did he want so many copies? It didn't matter. This was Biafra talking so I hopped to it. I sent the multiple copies he requested and weeks later a fat parcel from him appeared in my mailbox, beginning a friendship and correspondence that has lasted to this day. Fifteen years later over dinner, I told Biafra how much his letter meant to me. He almost looked embarrassed. Can you picture Biafra being embarrassed? He in turn told me how much he enjoyed the record.

Six or seven years after that terrible record review, the reviewer finally got back to me by email. He told me that he actually loved that sort of record and that his review was too harsh. I didn't respond to him. By that point, what I thought would be a one-off project had sprouted into a prolific label, distribution company, and record store. It was not what I had planned. One thing led to another, one record bled into another, months turned to years and there I was, smack in the middle. It was exactly what I wanted for a long time.

Flaming Midget after band practice, summer 1990, Palm City, FL. I'm in the middle. Photo by Paul Desario.

FLIPPER

GENERIC FLIPPER LP
SUBTERRANEAN RECORDS 1982

For a few years, I listened to a lot of Flipper. I did not listen to Flipper for entertainment. Flipper is uneasy listening music.

I was out of college, alone, alienated, and deeply unsatisfied with life. Flipper's creepy, monotone sludge and dark humor embodied the perfect soundtrack for my discontented early twenties. Square peg/round hole.

Night was particularly insular. I would remain cloistered in my room, stir-crazy and agitated, playing Flipper until I had to get out of the house. But there was nothing to do on the outside, either. So I would generally drive downtown, park my car somewhere, and walk empty streets for hours pondering all bullshit and honing my solitude. I became bitter and weird. In hindsight, it was a drag, but that's where I was then.

I often walked along the river and past the old drawbridge that divided our town into north and south. There was a park bench by the river where I could watch the boats, look at the stars and think myself stupid.

With time and self-examination, I grew more content. Things got better for me and Flipper stayed on the shelf collecting dust. Sometimes I'd pull out my well-worn copy of *Generic Flipper* just to look at it and remember how shitty things were at one time. But I could not bring myself to play it. Happy years passed without a single spin.

I'm glad I don't have that album on my shelf anymore. I don't want to go back to that. I did go back to look at my bench and it's not there anymore, either. Maybe that's good.

GAY COWBOYS IN BONDAGE
OWEN MARSHMALLOW STRIKES AGAIN 7"
SUBLAPSE RECORDS 1984

Jason was from Miami. He was a year older than the rest of us and cooler. He knew about stuff we didn't know about. He knew about real art and real music. He's one of the most talented, witty, charismatic people I have ever met. I still don't know why he isn't famous.

Jason knew about the Gay Cowboys in Bondage. I think he saw them play in Fort Lauderdale. Gay Cowboys were supposed to headline the first show I ever went to but they canceled at the last minute. I never got to see them.

Jason had the Gay Cowboys demo tape and the record. We all got dubbed copies. This was a staple of our crew's soundtrack for a few years. Gay Cowboys blasted in all of our bedrooms and in all of our first cars. Big Fred especially loved them.

The Gay Cowboys played silly, energetic music. A lot of the music from South Florida was goofy. The South Florida scene of my teenage years was mostly amiable. A lot of the band people were total geeks. There were a couple of jerks, not everyone was friends, but there were few problems with violence. It was a sharp contrast with Tampa's notoriously violent scene.

My Gay Cowboys tape and a lot of other good ones eventually met their demise in 1995 when I lost control of my van and drove into a drainage ditch. The van was flooded. The engine was ruined. I lost a lot of good music that I spent the next few years trying to replace.

A couple of years before I wrecked the van, I was in New York City with my band. It was my first trip to the city. We spent a lot of time at record stores. We checked out Reconstruction, Venus, and Bleeker Bob's. Bleeker Bob's was legendary—for overpricing. Even for NYC, their prices were high.

Somehow a copy of the Gay Cowboys 7" slipped under their radar and they underpriced it at five dollars. Unfortunately, Rob the Record Vulture saw it before I did. He didn't even want the record, but he snapped it up and showed it to me.

"Do you want this?"

"Yes!"

"Too bad! You'll get it from me someday!" Rob bought the record he didn't even want, that he knew I wanted, and lorded it over me.

Five years later, Rob wanted to go to Las Vegas but he didn't have any money. He asked me for a loan. He left a box of records as collateral because I never expected to be paid back.

To my surprise, Rob did pay me back. And he tossed in the Gay Cowboys record as interest on the loan. I was happy.

I played that Gay Cowboys record a lot and made a lot of dubs for friends.

One Saturday afternoon in 2004, my friend Phil walked into my record shop with a guy I didn't recognize. Phil introduced him to me as Eddie Nothing. Eddie was the bassist in both F and Gay Cowboys. I was pleased to meet him. I asked him about the possibility of putting out a Gay Cowboys CD with all of the recordings.

Sure, he said. That would be great. He seemed enthused. I took down his phone number but the idea went into hibernation for a couple more years.

Around 2006, I started getting serious about the project. I made several calls to Eddie and left messages but he never answered his phone and never returned my calls. I asked Phil about it. He said Eddie was not answering his calls either. Phil was worried.

I still wanted to do the project. I think it was Phil who put me in touch with singer Mike Lesser, better known as Milo. I left a weird message on his answering machine and didn't expect him to call back. Maybe a week later, he returned my call. His phone demeanor was exactly like his band demeanor. He was full of energy, spastic, and hilarious. I knew I would like working with this guy.

Milo sent me his personal copy of the demo, tons of old show flyers, magazine clippings, and band photos. All of the photos except one were black and white. I knew the sole color photo would have to be the cover shot. It was a great live pic of the whole band. I recognized it as the work of Leslie Wimmer.

Leslie had been half of the dynamic duo behind Open Records, one of the first independent record stores in South Florida as well as a groundbreaking record label. By 2006,

Leslie was running Blue Note, a record shop in Miami. I called and asked for permission to use the photo. She had no idea what photo I was talking about, but she gave me permission. I promised to send her a few copies of the CD.

Somehow I also got in touch with Barry Soltz who ran Sublapse Records, the label that released the Gay Cowboys 7" in 1984. I asked him for permission to reissue the music. He not only granted me permission, he sent me a mint copy of the record to use as a sound source. It was far cleaner than the copy Rob picked up in New York years earlier. Barry also wrote some great liner notes for the CD.

Malcolm Tent of the band Broken Talent got in on the act, too. He sent me a live recording of Gay Cowboys and more graphics for the packaging. I knew this CD was going to rock. I spent a couple of weeks doing the graphic design by hand, all razor and glue. It was a blast.

When the CD finally came out, I was really pleased with it. I sent Milo the copies I had promised him. He shared his copies with drummer Ravenous Gangrene. Guitarist Pete Moss had died about seven years earlier. That left me with the task of getting copies to Eddie Nothing.

I knew Eddie's real last name and used the Internet to find his address in Tampa. One night after closing the record shop, I drove to his apartment with 25 copies of the CD.

It was a part of Tampa I was not that familiar with. As I walked into the apartment complex, a neighbor stopped me and asked who I was looking for. He was just looking out for his neighbors. He pointed to the right door for me. I thanked him and knocked on the door.

Inside I could hear the hum of a television and someone moving around, I waited a long time with no response. I thought about knocking a second time. Just as I was about to knock, the door cracked open about four inches and Eddie's face appeared. He looked hesitant, maybe even suspicious.

"Eddie?"

"Yes?" He didn't remember me. It had been more than two years.

"Eddie, my name's Bob. Do you remember meeting me with Phil a couple of years ago at my record store?"

"Yes..." He was still hesitant.

"Do you remember me wanting to do a Gay Cowboys CD?"

"Yes..." Still leery.

"Well, it's done. Here's some copies for you."

"Oh." He was not that surprised. He had little reaction at all.

"So... here you go." I handed him the box.

"Uh, thanks." He still didn't seem that happy.

"If you'd like to tell me what you think about it, my email address and phone number are on the CD."

"Oh. OK. Thanks." He casually looked at the box.

I was expecting him to invite me in to talk, but he just said, "Bye" and closed the door. I didn't know what to make of it. I called Phil and related my story to him. Phil didn't understand it either.

A couple years passed without a word from Eddie. In February 2008, three friends and I drove to Miami for a reunion concert by South Florida punk legends the Eat. The audience was packed with Florida punk royalty. There were members of almost every important Florida band walking around, shaking hands and catching up with each other. Florida's godfather of rock 'n' roll, Charlie Pickett, was holding court at the bar. Flash, the singer of F, and I posed for a photo. Brian L., Pete, and I posed for a pic with all of the members of the Eat. The bassist of Rugged Edge came up to me and handed me three sealed copies of the band's rare 12". It was indeed a cool night.

I spied Leslie Wimmer across the room. It had been years since we'd last met. I re-introduced myself and she hugged me. I asked her how she liked the CD. She said she loved it and she hugged me again. I told her she was one of my record biz heroes. She told me that I was one of her heroes. This night was getting more awesome by the minute and the Eat had not even played yet.

Then I saw Eddie in the corner of the room. I didn't know if I should approach him. I had no idea what he was thinking. Finally I decided I should talk to him. I walked up, told him who I was, and he smiled broadly. He hugged me, too, and without any prompting he told me how much he loved the CD. I was glad to hear it.

Then the Eat came on and they were completely astounding. Eddie moved up front and went nuts the whole night, just like he did when he was a Gay Cowboy in Bondage.

GROSS NATIONAL PRODUCT
RONALD MCVOMIT'S
14 SONG HAPPY MEAL 7"
BACON TOWNE RECORDS 2006

Scott was new in town. Being a music addict, he found my record shop right away. But at first I was not sure I liked him. He was sarcastic and voiced strong opinions about any subject that came up. Many of his opinions were contrary to mine and he liked to debate. I did not like being challenged in my record store, my castle. I was, however, glad to take his money, which he spent freely.

Eventually, I became accustomed to his conversational style and began to find nuggets of wit. Soon we started talking about playing music together but we both wanted to be the drummer. We picked out a date to jam. I had a guitar and a bass, too. I figured we'd take turns on the various instruments and figure out who'd play what. But I really wanted to play drums.

We each came to practice with a few song ideas. It became obvious that Scott was a better drummer than me, so I yielded the kit to him. I took my position as bassist and we began writing songs.

I had not played bass with a band in fourteen years; it would be fun to revisit. I had a hard time keeping up with Scott. He wanted to play faster and faster. This forced me to get better quickly.

We found a guitarist and a singer who could not seem to make it on time to our 3:00 Sunday afternoon band practices. After a few frustrating Sundays, we replaced them with Adam and Marley, two teenagers who were dating each other. Scott was almost 30, I was 36 and was starting a new band with dating teenagers and an elementary school art teacher whom I had just met.

Adam was a good guitarist who took the skeletons of songs that Scott and I worked out and gave them muscle. Marley had never been in a band before and lacked confidence. Scott and I built her up with praise and pep talks and after a while, Marley found her stride and became magnetic on stage.

Marley had no idea what to sing about, so Scott and I wrote most of the lyrics. This is where Scott's opinions and sarcasm came in handy. He wrote clever, biting lyrics. Sometimes Scott or I would write some lyrics for a song and give them to Marley to complete.

"I don't know what to write," she'd always say, but she usually came up with something good.

Scott and I became competitive songwriting machines. Practice would start with us jamming the old songs to warm up and then we'd work on new ideas.

"I have three ideas this week!"

"Yeah? I have five!"

Our styles worked well together. Sometimes Scott or I would show up to practice with a complete song finished, music and lyrics. But more often, it was just pieces.

A lot of times these pieces fit together perfectly to make a new song, like when married couples finish each other's sentences. Adam would give his opinions and add his flourishes to round things out. And if inspiration struck, Marley would start scribbling down lyrics—then sheepishly ask us if they were any good. I liked these group efforts. I get a lot of satisfaction out of the songwriting process.

When we had about twelve minutes worth of music, we played our first show. It was a short set, but we kept the energy high. It was a formula we'd keep: Play a bunch of songs as fast as possible without stopping for breath. It was not an original formula, but it was effective. At a bar gig in Tampa, a noted jackass tried to heckle us but we never stopped between songs long enough for him to get a word out. We played fifteen songs in eighteen minutes without a pause. As we walked off stage, he tried to say some bullshit but nobody paid any attention to his drunken ass. Then he came up to me and told me we'd be better if we dropped the political lyrics.

After a few months of gigging, we made a demo tape. We made lots of copies and gave them to anyone who wanted one. We started getting a nice following locally. Part of this was because there was a lull in the local music scene. There were not many bands in operation and we offered people something to get behind.

A few people said that they didn't like Marley's voice, or that they didn't like female singers, so they didn't come to our gigs. Not liking Marley's voice was a matter of opinion, but to make a blanket statement about female singers in general was small-minded and pissed me off. We tried to keep this buzz from Marley, but I think she picked up on it a little. We just did our best to kick ass as much ass as possible. Scott pushed us to play faster and faster; the band continued to improve.

The demo tape landed in the hands of Heather and Marck at Bacon Towne Records, who wanted to turn it into a real record. The demo was good, but we were now capable of better. We told them we'd like to go into a real recording studio and re-record the same songs. They even gave us a little money to do it.

Around this time, Adam and Marley broke up and things got uncomfortable. Practices were a little tense. Scott and I wondered about the future of the band. We hoped they could be around each other long enough to make the record. To their credit, they pulled it off. I don't know what happened between them, but it took character for them to continue working together. I would not have handled it as well as they did.

With their wounds still fresh, we entered the studio for a marathon recording session, eighteen songs recorded and mixed in one long day. (Fourteen songs made it to the record.) The new recording came out so much better that none of us could listen to the demo any more. We'd gotten faster and tighter and Marley had grown as a vocalist.

Scott and I worked together on the packaging for the record. He designed the front cover and I did the back. It was similar to our songwriting efforts. Our styles blended well together. Everyone was pleased with the finished record.

Later, when Heather and Marck, the owners of Bacon Towne, got married they played one of our songs at their wedding reception. Marley and I attended; we looked at each other and laughed. It was strange to hear our high-speed thrash at a wedding reception.

Before the record came out, we were already working on a new batch of music. With Scott pushing us for faster, shorter songs, we set a goal of making a fifty-song album. It was absurd but completely possible. We had about a third of the material written when Scott abruptly announced he had to move back to Michigan. And like that, our band was over. It was a hell of a year, short and fast, just like our music.

Marley playing with Gross National Product, circa 2006.
Photographer unknown.

WHO: PAT AND BRIAN L.

It had been a very slow day at the record store. A few minutes before closing, four unfamiliar teenagers walked in and started piling up CDs. Each one had five or six CDs in his hands.

"Excellent," I thought, "Today won't be a loss."

As these four strangers were stacking up CDs, a teenage couple walked in and started browsing. I had no one in the shop all day and now I had six customers. Things were looking up.

Then one of the kids from the first group made a signal and the original four blasted for the door with armloads of CDs. Fuck. I didn't think the teenage couple was part of this, but I didn't know them either. I jumped over the sales counter and chased the first four across the parking lot, leaving the other two alone in the store. I didn't think to grab my gun. If I had, I probably would be in prison.

"Drop the CDs or all you motherfuckers die," I screamed as I chased them. I reached out for a fat kid with blond hair and snagged a bit of his shirt before he broke away. As soon as I touched him, he dropped all of his CDs and looked like he shat himself. The other kids dropped some of the discs, scattering them across the asphalt.

The four kids had a car waiting around the corner with the engine running. They dove through the back doors. I was right on their heels.

The driver had his window rolled down. I jumped through the front window, feet first, and kicked him in the side of the face with both feet. He didn't see it coming and made an "ooof" sound as I connected. I was perched on my left hip, half in/half out of the car, not really holding onto anything. I kept kicking that asshole in the face as he peeled out to make his getaway. His coward friends in the backseat did nothing to help him. They just said, "Oh, shit" over and over.

The car picked up speed, heading to the main street; I was still hanging halfway out of the car, kicking away. I had to make a decision: go along for the wild ride or get back to my unlocked store with two strangers inside. Not knowing the couple, I tucked and rolled to the asphalt. Somehow I didn't get a scratch on me.

I walked back to the store, picking up the CDs strewn all over the parking lot. By my estimate, they got away with maybe five or six. I recovered about a dozen.

In the store, the teenage couple was just standing there, doing nothing.

"Did you see that?" I asked.

"Yes," the guy said emotionlessly. That's how I met Pat.

By 1998, Pat and his brother, Brian L. were part of my innermost circle, working alongside Sam and Pete. Unlike the effusive Sam and Pete, these guys were solemn to the point of parody.

Ella used to call Pat, "Robot Pat." The first time she met him, I was out of the shop running errands. She came in and asked where I was.

"Out," was Pat's reply.

"OK, I'll sit down and wait for him."

Pat said nothing. Ella sat there in jagged silence for a few minutes until she said, "I'm Ella. I'm Bob's girlfriend."

To which Robot Pat deadpanned, "I know." End of conversation.

One time Brian L. arrived for his shift with a plastic bottle in his hand. Without betraying any emotion, he handed it to me and said, "Our dog died. Do you want this dog shampoo?" I thanked him and he got down to work. No more was said about the dead dog.

They are dudes of few words and carefully measured actions until they have a few drinks in them. Then you have no idea what will happen. Alcohol was not allowed at the store, so my only windows into Pat and Brian L's wild side were occasional road trips or other outside functions. The contrast was remarkable. The evening the store closed, Brian L. had spent much of the day drinking at the pub a few doors down. When he reported to duty, he was of little use as a worker but was great fun in the crowd during the live music portion of the evening. A couple of years later, an evening with Pat in New Orleans showed a man capable of Belushi-like consumption. It scared me, especially when he fell like a tree, passing out face first onto the sidewalk.

But for the most part, my hours with these brothers were no-nonsense affairs, full of punctuality, strong work ethic, and simple, declarative statements like, "I am finished with this," and "I'm leaving now." They could have been warmer with the customers—strike that—they *should* have been warmer with the customers, but it was not in their wiring. Nonetheless, I always knew that a shift with Pat or Brian L.

would be productive, efficient, and free of drama. If they had any bullshit going on in their lives, they checked it at the door. I used to joke that I wanted to clone these guys and have an army of perfect employees. I still say it; I'm just no longer joking.

They worked hard at the record store until the day the doors closed for good.

Pete, Lee Ving of the band Fear and Pat in front of the Brass Mug, Tampa, FL, 1998. Photo by Steve Western.

GUN CLUB
FIRE OF LOVE LP
SLASH RECORDS 1981

In 2011, I dove into the world of Internet radio. Characteristically, I went headfirst. I loved the possibilities of putting music on the Internet. There was no telling who would hear it or where. The potential was almost unlimited.

Internet broadcasting reminded me of all the mix tapes my friends and I traded. The idea was the same: Spread the music around. But with the Internet, you could reach hundreds, maybe thousands of people at the same time. Mix tapes were like hand grenades; Internet radio was like an atom bomb and I wanted to blow shit up.

I read a book, checked out a few websites, and got started. I put together my first podcast and posted it on a website. I picked a Gun Club song for the first set of music.

I first heard Gun Club back in 1983. A friend made me a tape of their first album, *Fire of Love*. I played the heck out of that tape. At some point the tape got lost or broken and many years passed without any Gun Club in my life. Finally I found my own copy on vinyl. As soon as I put it on, it all came back to me. It sounded as fresh and wild as it did back in 1983.

The first podcast had some of my favorite music, but it was a little dry. It is difficult for me to listen to. But it caught someone's ear, because after less than 48 hours, I got an offer to have my show carried on a large Internet radio station, multiplying my chances to be heard. A few weeks later, another Internet station picked me up. The chances multiplied again. I had weekly slots on two popular stations and the program was available on demand on my own website.

I was stoked. Each one hour program took me five hours to produce. Since I was putting so much work into it, I wanted it to be heard as many times as possible. It was also an ego thing—I liked the attention. Everyone who creates loves attention, whether they will admit it or not. Actors, comedians, writers, artists, musicians—they all want applause. I'm the same. I don't know why that is. It is kind of sad if you think about it.

My foray into Internet broadcasting lasted 46 weeks.

The more time I spent on my program, the more it distanced me from Ella. We didn't have a lot of time together and I was spending five hours a week on a hobby to satiate my piggish ego. As I worked on my episodes, I could see her watching me from across the room. She looked bored and lonely. I'd take off my headphones and tell her that I was almost finished. A lot of nights she went to bed before me. A few times she tried to engage me in conversation about my new hobby and I was brief with my answers. It did not interest her. She just wanted to talk to me. I was a fool.

Pete and me on the radio, July 2011.
Photo by Shane Hinton.

HATED YOUTH
HARDCORE RULES ᴛᴹ
BURRITO RECORDS 2000

During the infancy of the Internet, information was not as abundant as it is now. People were harder to track down. I heard a few songs on a compilation by a mystery band from Tallahassee named Hated Youth that piqued my interest for years. Who were these guys, and what else did they do? I wrote an online article about Florida punk rock that asked these very questions. One day, the answers walked through the front door of my record store.

A Hated Youth song had appeared on an unauthorized compilation album from Europe. Just a few days after I ran out of copies in the shop, a guy walked in asking for it. I told him I sold out and didn't think I could get more. The guy really needed a copy. He introduced himself as Gary Strickland, the singer of Hated Youth.

He was soft spoken, not at all like the voice of Hated Youth. Of course, seventeen years had passed. In that time, Gary drifted from punk rock but never stopped playing music. His newer music is decidedly more nuanced than Hated Youth's aural machine gun attacks. I showed him my personal copy of the European bootleg. He was not mad about being bootlegged. Rather, he was flattered. And absolutely bewildered. Who, he wondered, would pick one of his old songs for a bootleg and why?

By the early 2000s, a lot of early 1980s music was being reissued—sometimes illegitimately. As an archivist, I thought this was vital. As a record seller, these reissues were sure sellers. Which led me to my next question for Gary: Did Hated Youth have any unheard recordings? Yes, he said, as he handed me a very old cassette tape from his pocket. Hated Youth's complete 1983 recordings, thirteen songs in all. Ten had never been released, heard only by those closest to the band.

I snapped it into the cassette deck and pushed play. New Hated Youth songs—new to me, at least. Belligerent outbursts ripped from the speakers, escaping from the tape that held them captive for nearly two decades. This sort of rage is timeless. The world needed to hear this.

As we listened, Gary told me what each song was called. A few times, he quietly sang along with the tape, a wistful look in his eyes. Gary told me how the band started, why it ended, where they played, and practiced. He told me what the other members were up to. To me, this information was as important as the music.

For the second time in months, I found myself asking the singer of a long-defunct band for permission to make a record. Like the previous time, the reaction was quizzical. Why? Who would care? And like the last time, I assured Gary that the music was worth hearing. I convinced him that people would care. I felt strongly about documenting this unheard music before it was lost forever.

Gary didn't know for sure how many copies of the cassette were in existence, but he guessed it was not many. He said he might be able to find the original master tape, but after a few weeks of searching and phone calls, we gave up. I'd have to use his old tape to make the record. Unfortunately, one of the thirteen songs had a serious sound dropout and could not be used. If a good copy of that song exists, we have no idea where it is. We never found the master tape.

Gary ran the idea by the other members of the band. One of them was opposed—not to the music being released, but to *me* releasing it. He didn't know who I was—and why, he asked, should I be allowed to do it?

Who, Gary asked, should be allowed to release the music? The other guy had no answer. No one else had ever expressed interest in the band. Gary told him I was the right man for the job and the other guy gave his consent. I took the tape to a recording studio for restoration.

Gary and the other band members raided their closets for images I could use for the packaging. And he put me in touch with a man who'd photographed the band a few times. He still had the negatives from a 1982 show in Gainseville. I paid the photographer one hundred dollars to use three of his pictures. It was money well spent and these three images have since circulated across the Internet.

The record went to be one of my label's most popular titles. Two pressings sold out quickly. I would have made more copies, but the printer lost the cover art and I didn't want to re-design the packaging. But it doesn't matter. Digital versions of the record have spread like a rash all over the web. The music is still in circulation and that's what's important.

MDC
MILLIONS OF DEAD COPS LP
R. RADICAL RECORDS 1982

I had been listening to punk rock for less than a year when a guy in my neighborhood let me borrow the first MDC album. It was a shock. Maybe unnerving is the right word.

As MDC singer Dave Dictor said in the *American Hardcore* documentary, it was a big jump from the Ramones and "Hey, ho let's go!" to MDC's "Dead cops! Dead Cops!" It was far more radical than even the Dead Kennedys' fractured take on rock 'n' roll, far more intense than the Circle Jerks' snarky, Chuck-Berry-on-fire outbursts. I listened to the album on headphones, knowing damn well this was one I could not possibly explain to the folks. They were OK with the Ramones, they even liked a few songs, but how do you explain Millions of Dead Cops?

The lyrics pummeled me. It seemed like Dave Dictor was yelling right in my face, and he seemed so sure of what he was yelling. The lyric that especially unnerved me was, "And there's no God in heaven, so get off your knees." My parents raised me Catholic. I was young and sheltered; I thought everyone believed in God. What was this? A brain bomb.

I listened to the album a few times, made a tape copy, and returned it. I recall sneaking the record out of the house under my shirt. Could not let mom see that one. Nope.

The first few times I listened to my tape, I was still in shock at the lyrical directness—coupled with the musical sledgehammer of this mighty band at their peak. I have never stopped listening to this album. All these years later, there are times it still catches me off guard and gives me the chills.

Twenty years after that first spin, I sent an email to Dave Dictor telling him what a powerful effect the album had the first time I heard it. He never responded.

But a few months later, Dave called to see if I'd buy some MDC CDs for my store. Yes, of course. Then I mentioned that I let bands play in my record shop and that if MDC were ever in the area, I'd love to do a gig for them. Dave said, "OK, let's do that. How about April?"

We got to work and found MDC three Florida dates—Miami, Brandon, and Daytona. They flew into Miami, rented a car, drove from gig to gig, and flew back home.

The gig at my shop was a big deal. Every band in town wanted to play so we made it nine local bands with MDC headlining. The place was packed. I was sitting behind my drum kit, taking a break between songs, when this older guy squeezed his way through the crowd. He wiggled his way right up to the drum kit, leaned over, extended his hand, and said, "Bob? I'm Dave Dictor!" My face lit up. We shook hands and I announced into my microphone, "Alright! MDC is here!" The crowd went nuts.

After my set, I stood outside and talked to Dave for a little while. His eyes are piercing, as brilliant as his music. He's a very funny, very smart guy, too. He mentioned liking an article I'd written for a magazine. I was surprised that he even saw it.

After another band or two, MDC took the stage and from the first note to the last, it was pure energy. I'd seen MDC six years earlier in San Francisco with a different line up and they were terrible—easily the most disappointing thing I'd ever seen. I could not believe I walked out on MDC, but man, they sucked that night. Not so that sweltering day in Brandon. They were focused and flawless.

While MDC blasted through "Business on Parade," I thought of the ironic juxtaposition: The most radical band in the world playing in the back of a record store in a strip mall on the main drag of suburbia. Just a couple of hundred feet away, SUVs and luxury cars whizzed by on State Road 60 to the Brandon Mall, Best Buy, and Outback Steakhouse. It was perfect. Dave Dictor was a preacher, spewing forth fire and brimstone politics to lazy, complacent, comfortable, middle class kids who needed some intellectual shaking up.

By the time the band got to, "Dead Cops," the crowd was churning in frenzy. The audience shouted the chorus in a way that was almost as unnerving as the first time I'd heard this refrain on headphones back in high school. I could not help smiling as I sat on the P.A., watching the fervor. This was one of those serendipitous, affirming, self-actualizing moments when it felt like I was doing exactly the right thing with my life.

M.D.C

and 8 local bands   SAT APRIL 19, 3:00 PM $10 ALL AGES

at Sound Idea 113 East Brandon Blvd in Brandon (813) 653-2550

No smoking   No drinking   No morons

| M.D.C. | Lawnmowers Gone Awry | Anoxia | Reckless Beerhunters | Dancing Lepers |
| John Madden And The Electric Condoms | | DFC | Crotch Rotte | RunnAmucks |

PLEASE NOTE THE EARLY START TIME — 3:00 PM SHARP!

Flyer for Apr. 19, 2003 MDC concert at 113-H.
Flyer design by Bob Suren.

MEATMEN
WE'RE THE MEATMEN
...AND YOU SUCK! LP
TOUCH AND GO 1983

A few Meatmen songs made it onto a seminal mix tape that spread among my high school crowd, promulgating us in the aural aesthetic of early American hardcore. Hardcore took the original punk ethos to the extreme. Shorter, faster, louder, meaner. This mutant offspring of punk rock, this ugly fucking kid, took a lot of the original punks by surprise. It was too intense, too violent, too stupid, and too artless for many. A lot of the original punk rockers bailed and the scene moved on without them.

The Meatmen were decidedly hardcore. Unabashedly hardcore. Their barrage of barre chords and barking vocals was rude, crude, and obnoxious. It was perfect fodder for adolescent gonzos. My friends and I took to their din instantly.

In my sophomore year, I brought the aforementioned mix tape with me to a school function and cued it up to the Meatmen song, "Dumping Ground," a particularly foul number. We were building floats for the homecoming parade. I asked a teacher if I could play some music. When she said yes, I hit play and singer Tesco Vee's voice filled the hall with his vulgarity-laden pre-song monologue. Everyone stared at me. Three people started laughing. The rest were shocked. The teacher scowled, ran over to me, and hit stop.

"That was not funny. You better leave now."

So, I left. I was not a troublemaker. That was out of character for me. I don't know why I did it—for a laugh?

We continued to adore the Meatmen and they continued to make records. And although their style changed over the next couple of years, the over-the-top raunchy humor remained. Indeed, it became more outrageous on each record. When my friends and I started playing music, the Meatmen were a heavy influence.

I began writing letters to Tesco. Once, he sent a racy postcard with some filthy inscription on the back—something about needing an enema. My mom intercepted the postcard and was not happy about it. She already was not too keen on the whole punk rock thing. She gave me another chiding about being a nice boy. I was a nice boy; I just liked my music a little aggressive.

Fast forward a couple of years from my prank. The phone rang at our house; my mom answered it. The caller asked for "Bob," so she handed it to my dad. After a few seconds of confusion, my dad said, "I don't know what the hell you're talking about. I think you want my son." He handed it to me and said, "It's some idiot for you." (I am pretty sure he said this loud enough for the caller to hear.) It was Meatmen guitarist Lyle Preslar, who had also been in my old favorite Minor Threat!

Lyle said the Meatmen were coming to Florida and he wanted to know where to play. He heard Tampa was too violent but they might be willing to play there anyway. I was living in another part of the state but word of Tampa's recent problems with violence had reached me and I confirmed Lyle's concern.

I told him about the Cameo Theatre in Miami and gave him the phone number from a flyer I had. I also told him that Orlando might be worth a shot. He thanked me and I asked a few questions about the Meatmen and Minor Threat. Lyle said he'd let me know if any of the info worked out.

I never did hear from Lyle again, but Tesco wrote to tell me that they arranged three Florida shows for April 1986. He told me he'd get me in if I wanted to go. Unfortunately, due to parental issues, I couldn't make any of the concerts.

But Tesco and I stayed in touch and the next year the Meatmen planned to return to Florida in July, touring for their new album, *Rock 'N' Roll Juggernaut*. By then, I was playing in my second or third band. I told Tesco about us and he seemed genuinely interested. He said he'd put in a good word for us at the Cameo Theatre but we'd have to talk to the venue to get on the show.

We contacted the Cameo, sent a tape, and were invited to play July 4, 1987 with the Meatmen.

Jacksonville's Stevie Stiletto and the Switchblades jumped on the show at the last moment. And even though they were a known band with real records out and we were just a bunch of nobodies, they had to play first. I had their records and knew the songs. It was an added bonus to see them. They were killer.

Then we played and we were not killer. The crowd hated us. I am not even going to tell you the name of our band. For some reason, someone in our band—to be clear, not me—thought it would be funny to have a sandwich maker on stage. So, we had a guy in an apron at stage left with a small folding table building submarine sandwiches and handing them to the crowd. The sandwiches were hurled back at us. There was bread, mustard, cheese, pickles and lunchmeat all over the stage. A mustard-smeared slice of baloney plopped on our drummer's left thigh. After the punks ran out of sandwiches to throw, they began throwing full cans of garbage at us. I can laugh at this now, but at the time it was an embarrassment.

One of the songs in our set was a cover of "Ballroom Blitz," by the Sweet. We somehow played this song pretty well. When we played it that night, the garbage throwing slowed down for a couple of minutes. Then it resumed. We left the stage in shame. We fucked up our big show.

I went to sit on the curb by the loading door. Ray McKelvey, the singer of Stevie Stiletto and the Switchblades, was out there smoking a cigarette.

"Rough crowd," he said. And then he consoled me, telling me that any band could have a bad night. I told him we were usually good. I think my voice was weak and pathetic. But Ray was cool. He said we'd kill them next time. Ray passed away in 2013, just days after I wrote this.

I went back inside the club and headed to the lobby where the Meatmen were selling merchandise. When Tesco saw me, he came out from behind the merchandise table and walked toward me quickly with a big smile, right hand extended for a handshake. He liked us. As we shook hands there in the lobby of the Cameo Theatre, he told me, "Killer version of 'Ballroom Blitz.'"

"Are you a Sweet fan?" I asked.

"Oh, yeah. Big time." His smile was still there. We were OK with Tesco. I felt a lot better about our performance.

The Meatmen played after midnight and were brilliant in every capacity. It was one of the best concerts I've ever seen. For years my band mates and I referred to the summer of 1987 as Meatmen Summer. I've lost touch with most of them, but I've stayed in touch with Tesco.

Tesco Vee at Blue Chair Music, Tampa, FL, 1995. Photo by Bob Suren.

MINOR THREAT
OUT OF STEP LP
DISCHORD RECORDS 1983

A bunch of us were driving around in Brian B's Pontiac Sunbird, going from skate spot to skate spot where we'd shred until we got bored or chased off by chubby, middle-aged store owners or actual cops. Small town punks. What else was there to do? It was a time when skating and punk rock were enmeshed. If you were a punk, you probably skated. If you skated, you definitely listened to punk. What else was there to skate to? Huey Lewis and the News? REO Speedwagon?

The compilation *This Is Boston Not L.A.* had been in heavy rotation all day. After the third or fourth spin, Dave Rat said, "Have you heard the new Minor Threat?"

New Minor Threat? We had not heard it, but it was Minor Threat and it was new, so please crank that fucker, Dave Rat. Of course by the time the "new" Minor Threat made it to our small town, it was probably a year and a half old. The music circulated slower then. It was harder to find and people appreciated it more. Scoring a great record was cause for celebration and that great record inevitably was dubbed for everyone in the crowd.

For the past year or so, I had been blasting the shit out of the first two Minor Threat 7"s. The first time I heard the opening barre chord to "Filler" is the closest thing I'll ever have to a religious experience. Pure power and adrenaline. I got goose bumps on that first spin. There are times I still do if I am listening closely. Listening on headphones, it was as if singer Ian MacKaye was right there in the room, barking imperatives in my ear. It was and is essential music. And now Dave says there is more? Turn it up—fucking pronto.

Dave snapped *Out of Step* into the tape deck and we were knocked back by the powerful opening of "Betray." The music was slower and a little more melodic, but still very intense. This record alienated a lot of old fans. I have seen mixed reviews of it in old magazines. Some old timers still put it down. It is such a departure from the earlier work that some people unfairly wrote it off.

Not me. I grabbed the first copy I saw and held onto it for something like 27 years. I hunted down almost all of the cover variations, including the UK and German versions. It quickly became my favorite album and remained in the number one spot for many years; to this day it remains high on my list. We listened to *Out of Step* all the way through and when it ended we were quiet. That astounding music made four teenage skaters jacked up on Dr. Pepper and chocolate shut up momentarily. Then Dave said, "It's too bad they just broke up."

We were stunned. Of course, the break up was maybe a year and a half earlier, but the news just made it to us. Dave was our grapevine to the rest of the punk rock universe. And now he had stunned us. It was like hearing that someone famous had died. Dave said it was because one of the guys went off to college. It was the first time I thought of a band as a group of real people and a thing that could just stop. I mean, the Rolling Stones started before I was born and they're still going. It never occurred to me that bands end. And for such mundane reasons.

In the book *American Hardcore*, Meatmen singer Tesco Vee calls Minor Threat, "...lightning in a bottle." He calls it a chemistry that cannot be contrived. We played the tape and skated until the sugar wore off and the sun went down.

MISFITS
DIE, DIE, MY DARLING 12"
PLAN 9 RECORDS 1984

During my senior year of high school, a record store opened a few miles from my house. Previously, the only record store in town was some crappy place called Tape Exchange or something that was in a strip mall. That place was good for AC/DC tapes and... um, nothing else.

The new place was Confusion Records. Confusion Records was aptly named. For many years, there seemed to be no logic to the product placement. Most record stores alphabetize. Confusion appeared to be organized by smell or molecular weight or by the color of the records' auras or something.

Owner John Clements is, like me, a graduate of the University of Florida. Unlike me, I think John ingested more than his share of recreational pharmaceuticals in the 1970s. And unlike me, John worked the Jungle Cruise at Disney World after college. John used to be a substitute teacher at my high school. For a long time, John lived in a trailer on a lychee farm next door to the school. Before he had a record shop, he peddled vinyl out of the back of a station wagon at the flea market. His favorite bands were the Beatles, the Rolling Stones, Sonic Youth, and Eurythmics. He was the first vegetarian I ever met.

I bought a lot of records at Confusion over the years, but *Die, Die My Darling* was the first one. I remember it clearly because I was a total dick.

John was selling the record for eight bucks, which I did not think was fair because there were only three songs on it. I arrogantly pointed this out to him and asked for a discount.

John flipped the record over and looked at the three song titles. Then he played it off like it was a full-length album.

"No," he said, "That's just like a saying, those aren't the song titles." That didn't even make sense. I don't know if he really believed that or not, but it was fairly obvious that they were the song titles and that there were only three of them. I told him I would buy the record for six dollars and he grudgingly agreed. Sorry, John. I hope my repeat business over the years more than made up for that.

After that bumpy start, John and I got along fine and still do, even though it has been more than a decade since I have seen him in person.

I began hanging out at Confusion Records whenever I could. Even when I didn't have money, I would go there and talk with John. Talking with John is the best part of Confusion Records because you never know where the conversation is going to go. Sometimes John changes subjects in midsentence. He may start a sentence talking about a record and end the sentence talking about food. Or UFOs. Or the Carter Administration. You never fucking know. John's mind is like an endless Butthole Surfers song. And I think he would like that simile.

It took John about two years to get a phone hooked up at Confusion. By this time, John and I had become kind of tight. Sometimes he'd leave me in charge of the store while he took off on his bike for food or cigarettes or to run to the bank. Nobody ever came in and bought anything while he was gone, but it was fun being in charge for a little while. A few times I got to answer the phone.

I pushed John to stock more punk records. There were a few other punk rockers left in town from my high school days. I told him a few bands he should look for. I think I talked him into ordering from Dischord Records. He picked up what he could and I think he did pretty well with the punk stuff.

I also begged John to carry *Maximum Rocknroll* magazine. I could not find it anywhere. I could have subscribed, but I liked picking it up in stores. It felt more real. So, John started stocking *Maximum Rocknroll*. He ordered three copies every month. I always got one. I never figured out who bought the other two copies.

Sometimes people would come into Confusion Records and ask to use the toilet. Unless John knew the person, he usually said the toilet was broken. John let me use the toilet. One time there was no toilet paper and I needed it. There were stacks of old magazines. There were several dog-eared paperbacks. There was an ominous claw hammer. There was an open jar of peanut butter with a knife in it. But no toilet paper.

"John," I said from inside, "Do you have any toilet paper?"

No response.

I called out again, "John, I need some toilet paper, please."

No response.

I hiked up my pants and shambled out of the bathroom in a half-crouch.

"John, do you have any toilet paper?"

John looked at me like I was speaking Venusian. I asked again and gave up. He was zoned out. I went into the bathroom and weighed my options. The claw hammer was out of the question. I figured something out, cleaned myself up, and walked out of the bathroom. I never did figure out what that was all about.

When I learned to screen print, I made a batch of baby blue T-shirts that read, "Confusion Records: Home of the Broken Toilet." He liked that.

And when I put out my first record, Confusion was the first place I brought it. I wanted the local shop to carry my record, the shop where I discovered so many great things. John took three copies. On consignment. For three years. One sold.

Several years later when I was running my own shop, Phil Vane, the late singer of Extreme Noise Terror, tried to haggle me down on a twelve-dollar CD. I thought of John and gave him a two-dollar discount.

John Clements wearing the "Home of the Broken Toilet" T-shirt at the original Confusion Records, mid 1990s.

MISFITS
WALK AMONG US LP
SLASH RECORDS 1982

Just about everybody loves the Misfits. And everyone who does has strong opinions: favorite records; favorite songs; favorite lineups. *Walk Among Us* is probably my favorite. It is hard to choose definitively, but I have sentimental reasons for liking this one. It was the first Misfits I'd heard, but there is more to it.

Most punks in our area opted for the early U.S. hardcore look: T-shirts and torn jeans. Chuck Taylors for daily wear and combat boots for gigs. And then there was Dave Rat. Dave looked like he jumped off the back of an old Brit punk album, 365 days a year. He wore a studded leather jacket and heavy boots every day, even in the oppressive south Florida heat. He wore his blond hair charged and was the first guy I ever saw with an earring. And a nose ring! This was the early 1980s in a very "normal" town.

I had been into punk for a few months and had questions. I wanted to know where to get the music and where I could see these bands live. One of my friends suggested that I talk to Dave Rat. I was a little scared. Dave looked like a scary guy; I assumed he was mean. My friend introduced me. He was gregarious and articulate.

In the early 1980s it felt like punk rock was a youth culture. It really did feel like it was "us" against "them." It felt like this new music could change things. So Dave was very excited that there was a new face on his side. During that first talk in the crowded hall by the cafeteria, Dave bombarded me with names of bands, names of people, names of magazines, and names of cities with good scenes. It was the first time I ever heard the term "scene."

He told me that Tampa had a good scene. He went there often for gigs and wanted to move there.

A day or two later, Dave surprised me in the hall, very near the same spot where we first met, with a clutch of records and tapes. There was D.O.A., 7 Seconds, Buzzcocks, Peter and the Test Tube Babies, G.B.H., and more. The records, he told me, he wanted back. But the tapes were mine to keep. I was surprised he even remembered my name. How cool was this guy?

Well, one of those records was *Walk Among Us*, which was prominently placed at the top of the stack. Dave told me it was one of the best records ever. It was the first one I listened to when I went home that day.

Over the next couple of years, Dave and I hung out a number of times. (I still smile when I think of him riding his huge Sims "Screamer" skateboard in combat boots.) We were never best friends but he always accepted me, even though I was not nearly as "punk" as him. I never knew him to look down on anyone.

Dave continued making weekend excursions to Tampa and would regale us with tales of the bands he'd seen, the records he bought, and the people he met. He never seemed like he was bragging; he was filling us in. He made Tampa seem like Punk Utopia. In his junior year, he moved there and most of us in Martin County lost touch with him.

By 1995, I was living in the Tampa area, running my punk rock record shop and playing in a band. I often wondered about Dave, whether he was still in the area. A mutual friend told me that he was and tried to put me in touch with him. I wanted to tell him what a great push he gave me when I was first getting into punk and show him how far it took me. I made a few attempts to reach him and gave up.

In October 2004, Dave Rat was trying to break up a fight at a punk show in Tampa and was stabbed to death. He died trying to be a good guy.

Dave Rat in front of the tennis courts at Martin County High School in Stuart, FL, 1983. Courtesy of Christine Claybrook-Lumsden.

NEGATIVE APPROACH
S/T 7"
TOUCH AND GO 1982

Correspondence was always a giant part of punk rock for me. For decades, I got letters and parcels from around the world. Checking the mail was the best part of my day. In my first year of college, I began writing to a guy named BB. He was part of the busy punk rock pen pal group and so was I, so it was inevitable that we would eventually trade letters. He wrote to me first, for reasons I don't remember, and we hit it off.

Besides collecting vinyl, BB was also a tape trader, part of a small but dedicated niche of the music world. There are a lot of interesting recordings that are only available on cassette. These are mostly live concerts, band rehearsals, and demo recordings. People like BB are fanatical about finding these artifacts because they offer something less polished, more primal, and sometimes way better than the band's official studio releases. Tape traders are serious fans.

BB would send me long, photocopied lists of all the rare cassette recordings he had. Much of it was so arcane that I didn't know what I was looking at. But there were plenty of my favorites, too. BB was happy to copy anything for anyone if he got something in return. His tastes were far more esoteric than mine and I never had anything to offer that he did not already have. BB let me compensate him with blank tapes, cash, and postage stamps.

After eight or ten years, BB and I fell out of touch. Following a year or two of silence, I called to see how he was. It took him by surprise. He seemed a little uneasy on the phone. I invited him to visit me but he declined. Something was weird.

I mentioned this to a mutual friend. He told me that BB went through a devastating divorce that left him in financial and emotional ruin. A little after I heard the bad news, I got a letter from BB. He didn't explain his personal situation, but he told me he was selling his whole record collection. He said his best friend would get first shot at it and if I was interested, I could be next in line. I wrote back telling him I was very interested. I could not believe he was selling his records. A few weeks later, he sent a long, handwritten list of records.

He had some truly amazing stuff. He had records I'd never seen anywhere and records I'd never even heard of. And his prices were unbelievably low. He included a letter that said, "I'm not stupid. I know what these records are worth, but I want them to go to someone who will appreciate them. When you are finished with the list, please send it back as it is the only copy."

I showed the list to two of my friends. The three of us picked out the stuff we wanted and I sent BB the collective payment. A week or two later, the records showed up. They were in pristine condition. By this time, I'd saved up a few more bucks so I fired off another order to BB and returned his list.

Out of all the items that I got from him, the Negative Approach record was my favorite and the most valuable. I played it over and over. And I still can't believe I got it so cheaply. Until recently, I couldn't understand why BB got rid of everything.

Negative Approach singer John Brannon and I having
a mean face contest, 2012. Photographer unknown.

PILLSBURY HARDCORE
IN A STRAIGHTEDGE LIMBO 7"
FARTBLOSSOM RECORDS 1985

Because most record stores in the 80s didn't carry much punk rock stuff, people with an esoteric craving had to resort to mail order. Once I'd absorbed as much of the "big name" bands as I could find in local shops, I became a mail order addict. One of my favorite mail order operations was Toxic Shock, a record store in Pomona, CA, which boosted its income peddling vinyl through the mail—and still does to this day, although now based in Tucson, operating under the Westworld moniker.

I was used to ordering a couple of records at a time directly from my favorite record labels—Subterranean, Dischord, and B.Y.O. But one day the Reverend Fucking Mike Anarchy brought to school a fat, yellow Toxic Shock catalog. My friends and I gathered around a desk oohing and ahhing over the massive selection of old favorites and potential new favorites. The best part of the Toxic Shock catalog was the descriptions for each item. "Blazing thrash from Italy" or "Fast and furious Finnish hardcore." Punk rock from Brazil? Sweden? Indiana? Toxic Shock seemingly had it all. There were even a few bands from Florida, my home state, which I absolutely had to pick up.

We each circled the things we wanted and figured up our total. A day or two later we all brought in our money, dumped it on the desk and looked at it. We didn't know what to do. But we did know that we couldn't just send one hundred and sixteen dollars in cash and coins through the mail. We were probably too stupid to know what a money order was and of course none of us had a credit card. I volunteered to take the money home and have my mom write a check.

Naturally my mom wanted to know exactly what the hell "Toxic Shock" was and what the hell she was writing a check for. I didn't want it to come to this, but I sheepishly showed her the list of records that my friends and I picked out. We selected such classics as: Dayglo Abortions, Discharge, Hagar the Womb, Motörhead, Scared Straight, Justice League, Anti-Scrunti Faction, Roach Motel, Sewer Zombies, Blood Farmers, Permanent Scar, and, of course, Pillsbury Hardcore. I will never forget the uneasy look on my mother's face as she read the list. As she reached for her checkbook, she said, "You're a nice boy, Bobby. I hope this music doesn't change you."

Of course, the music did change me. I think it made me a better, stronger, funnier, more critical person and it has given me some of the greatest moments of my life. And I still think I am a nice boy.

Six or seven years later I started my own record label. The first place I thought of for distribution was Toxic Shock. I sent them a sample as they requested and never heard back. After a couple of months, I called and asked about it. I spoke to Bill Sassenberger, owner of Toxic Shock. He very gently told me that the record was not something he wanted to carry but to please keep him in mind. I was kind of crushed. Toxic Shock was the main place I wanted my record sold and it was not good enough. Shit.

But I did keep Toxic Shock in mind and two years later Bill Sassenberger decided to pick up my third release, beginning a working relationship that lasted fifteen years. I'm out of the music business, but as of this writing, Bill is in his thirty-third year. When I began my own mail order operation in 1993, I based it on what I learned buying from places like Toxic Shock. I am glad Sassy is hanging in there. He's a lifer.

In 2012 I was running a weekly podcast. In one episode, I did a tribute to Toxic Shock and played a set of records that I purchased from there, including Pillsbury Hardcore, one of my go-to records. One of the people who heard the podcast was Bill Tuck, the singer of Pillsbury Hardcore, who quickly got in touch to thank me for remembering his band. He also informed me that he used to work at Toxic Shock and that he may have packed a few of my orders. Bill Tuck continues to play music. And I am sure it has changed him for the better as well.

RAMONES
IT'S ALIVE 2XLP
SIRE RECORDS 1979

Ramones says it all, doesn't it? I suppose I could stop now, but I can't help myself. *It's Alive* is probably my favorite Ramones album. It is weird to pick a live album, but this one has so much energy and sentimental value. It was the first Ramones record I heard and the first punk rock record I ever heard.

My dad had a big record collection. I was always digging through it for new sounds. I was well acquainted with Buddy Holly, Little Richard, Elvis Presley, Chuck Berry, Fats Domino, and Jerry Lee Lewis before I even started school. He also had tons of doo-wop, which I still love, and all of those early 60s girl groups like the Chiffons, the Dixie Cups, the Marvelettes, the Shangri-Las, and the Supremes. I grew up on music, but it wasn't my own music. It was my dad's. Music from before I was born.

By middle school I was choosing my own music and getting turned onto music by friends. Our music. My soundtrack for a few years was AC/DC, Black Sabbath, Blue Oyster Cult, and Cheap Trick. But one day as I was digging through my dad's record collection, a record I had never seen before caught my eye: *It's Alive*.

The record was not in my dad's collection. It was at the front of a small stack of records, leaning against a wall, clearly separated from my dad's stuff. I was familiar with the other records but not this one. I have two older sisters, but I don't think either one of them bought it. Maybe one of their friends brought it over. I never did find out where it came from, but there it was. I spun it and *wow!*

The Ramones had some of the same pop melodies and rock 'n' roll structures that I was conversant with, but there was so much more energy and speed. These guys never stopped between songs. It was the musical equivalent of running full speed down a steep hill. I was instantly sold, especially by "Rockaway Beach."

I played it for my oldest sister and she loved it, too. Like me, she had no idea why the record was in our living room. We made a tape of it and listened to it in her car every time we drove somewhere. In a matter of days, we had the thing memorized, including all of Joey Ramone's sardonic stage banter.

I plunged headfirst into punk rock. My sister dabbled with a couple of bands but never made the full commitment. But she still loved the Ramones. Four or five years later she burst into my room to tell me that the Ramones were playing in Miami, just a couple of hours away.

I had never been to a concert with my sister and was a little scared to hang out with her because she's a bit of a maniac. But this was my big chance to see the Ramones. I had to do it. I asked her if I could bring a couple of friends. She said yes and we bought our tickets.

On the big day, my friends and I dropped by my sister's apartment and found that she had cooked dinner for us. It looked awful. My friends didn't want to eat it and made some excuse. This agitated my sister and she made a pissy remark. My friends were terrified of her. The night was off to a weird start.

I ate some of the food and then it was time to go. My sister drove; she is a terrible driver. She has bad eyesight and is easily distracted. And she likes to drink. She cracked a couple on the way to Miami but remained in control—for a while.

We got to the Cameo Theatre on Miami Beach, grabbed some good seats, and waited for the show to start. The Dickies were supposed to be the opening band, which my friends and I were chuffed to see, but they'd dropped off the tour a couple of days earlier. The promoter scrambled to find a local replacement and came up with the Miami band Amazing Grace. I thought they were pretty good. My sister hated them. She booed them and threw things at them all night.

"Who the fuck is this trying to play?" she asked me.

"Amazing Grace..."

"Well, they suck! You guys suck! Fuck you guys!"

My friends' trepidation grew; my sister continued drinking. Eventually the Ramones came on.

The Ramones were beyond awesome. I think "Ramones" should become a superlative in every language on earth. They played every song I wanted to hear. They did four encores; each encore was four songs. They went on around midnight and left the stage around 2 A.M. This remains the greatest concert I have ever seen.

We found our way back to the car. My sister had a few beers during the concert but was OK to drive. We hit I-95 north back to Stuart, talking about the greatness we had just witnessed. It was very late. And then my sister said, "So what do you want to do now?"

We wanted to go home. It was getting close to 3:00 in the morning and we still had quite a way to drive. My sister insisted that she was taking us to an all-night go-kart track in Fort Lauderdale—her treat! My friends were clearly shaken.

We pulled into the go-kart place as the three of us repeatedly told my sister that we were not up for it, but she insisted it would be "fun." My friends looked worried.

My sister stormed up to the ticket window and bought four tickets. Then she turned around to hand them to us and my friends and I just shook our heads.

"What? Really? You guys don't want to do this? Fuck it. I'll get the money back."

The person working the counter refused to give my sister her money back. She started yelling and pounding on the glass. There were maybe six or eight people in line behind her waiting for tickets, getting very scared.

Finally my sister told the poor ticket person to fuck off, spun around to the next guy in line and tried to give him the tickets. He wouldn't take them.

"Here, take these fucking tickets. They're free, asshole!"

The guy backed off. My sister tried the next guy in line but he didn't want any free tickets from the crazy lady either. By this time, someone had called the police.

A big Florida State Trooper tapped my sister on the shoulder from behind. She didn't know who it was, but that didn't stop her from spinning around and shoving whoever it was. I can still hear her palms thumping on that cop's chest and screaming, "What?!"

To his credit, the cop was extremely restrained. He held my sister's wrists and told her to calm down. She did calm down a little. The cop turned to the crowd and said, "Who is with this woman?"

I raised my hand and said, "She's my sister." The whole crowd was looking at me. My cheeks reddened.

"Please take your sister home or she is going to jail."

"OK."

"Do you drive?"

"Yes."

"You drive, not her."

"OK."

We left. But my sister refused to let me drive. I think my friends had crapped their pants at least twice by then. Somehow we made it home. My sister said that the Ramones rocked but my friends were pussies. Next to my sister, everyone was a pussy. (A year later she forced me into stowing away on a cruise ship.)

In 2001, I was visiting one of my punk rock buddies in Amsterdam. It was a Sunday morning. I had several hours to kill before my plane home. My buddy told me there was a tribute to the Ramones that afternoon in a local bar. Hey, ho, let's go!

At the bar, a big fat guy and a skinny guy in Ramones garb took the stage with acoustic guitars and blasted through twenty or thirty Ramones songs, campfire style. It was excellent. The whole audience was singing every word. People were laughing and dancing. It was a real mixed crowd, older and younger people, people of all different backgrounds, singing and dancing to the Ramones. It was puissant evidence of the great band's universal appeal.

My friend introduced me to several people at the bar; every single one of them seemed genuinely pleased to meet me. I shook a lot of hands, met a lot of fellow Ramones fans. Then it was time for me to head to Schiphol and catch my plane home.

I was in Atlanta, waiting for my connecting flight back to Tampa when I heard Ramones music blasting from somewhere. I looked around and discovered it was coming from a big screen TV. Why was "Blitzkrieg Bop" on CNN? Then I saw it. Joey Ramone had died. There was a picture of him in the corner of the screen. I put two and two together: The tribute in Amsterdam a few hours earlier was for him. Nobody said anything about Joey dying. Everyone there knew but me. Shit.

That copy of *It's Alive* sat in my parents' living room for at least a year. I never knew how it got there. Then one day I went to listen to it and it was gone. Just gone. As mysteriously as it had appeared, it disappeared. Here today, gone tomorrow.

The legendary Cameo Theatre in Miami Beach as it looks today. Photo by Bob Suren.

WHO: EDGAR AND OLIVER

Ella and I decided we didn't want kids. We wanted dogs. Ella wanted basset hounds. She found a lady selling a litter of basset pups so we went for a look. There were seven or eight of the little things, rolling around in straw on the floor of a barn. They were impossible to resist.

We picked the two boys in the litter. One was timid and scared of us. He tried to hide behind the lady's legs. That was Edgar and he was always a big baby about everything. The other boy pup had a perfectly round, black spot on his side. It looked like an eight ball. That was Oliver.

We paid the lady, scooped the boys up, and put them in a box for the ride home. Edgar cried the whole way. Oliver seemed pretty cool.

There was a period of adjustment. At first I was not sure I'd like having dogs. Edgar yapped and whined constantly. Both of them made messes all over. And for a few days it seemed like I was allergic to them. After a while, my sneezes and itchy eyes stopped. And eventually, the boys calmed down and made most of their messes outside.

After maybe a week, I started taking them to work with me at the record store. I felt bad leaving them home alone all day. So, every day I loaded them into their doggie crates in my van and we made the 30-minute ride to work. Oliver liked riding in the crate. He'd lie down and relax. Edgar never learned to relax in the crate. He'd stand up the whole time, panting, and looking at me with desperation.

They claimed the couch in the storage room as their territory and I laid down newspaper for their doggie business. For the next eight years, the record store smelled like basset hounds and their hair got all over everything. I did not know they shed so much. The *St. Petersburg Times* ran an article about the shop that began, "Punk rock smells like basset hounds." We had a good laugh over that.

Most of the customers loved the dogs. And the dogs loved the attention. Almost everybody petted them. They loved going to work and seeing the regular customers. I used to ask them, "Who do you think we'll see today? Jarrod? Emily? Bridget? Phillip?" Then they'd get all excited, thinking about their work buddies. But their favorite work buddy was Pete, my employee. They loved all of my helpers, but Pete drove them mad. He would roll all over the floor with them. Edgar would bark so much that his mouth would get frothy. Oliver would run around Pete in circles, moaning and howling.

My landlord did not like the dogs. He didn't come around very much. Sometimes years would pass without a visit. One day he showed up to the shop and saw the dogs for the first time.

"I didn't know you had dogs. I wouldn't have rented to you if I knew you were going to bring dogs."

I told him that the dogs were well behaved and that they did most of their business outside before and after work. Just as I was saying this, Oliver jumped off the couch, strutted out to the middle of the floor and pissed all over the place.

"For God's sake, he's peeing right now!" the landlord said with heavy disgust.

When the store closed and I began working from home, the dogs seemed confused. They didn't know why they didn't ride in the van anymore. They missed their smelly couch and their work buddies. They got bored and Oliver started picking fights with his brother. For a while, we had to keep them separated.

Ella and I bonded with the boys quickly. I think I fell for them harder than she, because one time she said to me, "They are just dogs. I love them, but you treat them like children. When they die, you're going to be crushed." She said I loved too much, but what was I going to do—hold back? I took the risk and gave the pups my full devotion. I felt it was worth the eventual crush.

The dogs and me at work, circa 2002. Photographer unknown.

RATTUS
USKONTO ON VAARA LP
NEW FACE RECORDS 1985

As I got deeper into punk rock, I became more interested in music from other countries. Punk rock felt like a stance, a counter-culture, a family of people I'd never met in places I'd never see. Somehow we were connected, distant relatives with common ancestors in the Ramones. Knowing that there were like-minded people around the globe was galvanic. I was fascinated by this notion. One band famously coined the term, "A Network of Friends." It was apropos.

Finland seemed to have an endless supply of amazing bands with unpronounceable names like Maanalainen Pelastrusarmeija, Aivoproteesi, and Kansanturvamusiikkikomissio. I didn't know what these bands were singing about, but I knew we were on the same side of the fence. We were allied. I knew anything from Finland was going to be great. At the top of my list of Finnish favorites was Rattus.

Rattus formed in 1978. As far as I knew, they broke up around 1988. But one day in 2004, I was on the Internet and saw photos of a Rattus reunion show. They were playing again with all original members. I found a contact email and quickly fired off a rabid fan letter, mentioning that if Rattus ever wanted to play in Florida, I'd be happy to help with a show.

I got an instant response, but perhaps there was a little language barrier, because the email said something like, "Of course we can't come to the United States for just one show."

This was from the band's manager since 1978, Vote Vasko, tireless archivist and primary photographer of Finland's golden age of punk. If you have any Finnish punk rock records, Vote probably took the band photos on them. Vote also wrote numerous articles about Finnish bands for publications around the world and ran his own record label. His work has made him, without a doubt, the most important person in the history of Finnish punk.

I wrote back to Vote saying that I knew the band couldn't come for just one show and stressed the "if" part of my initial offer. His response was something like, "We'll come for two weeks. We'll start the tour in New York City." Huh? I guess Vote was asking me (or telling me) to book a tour for Rattus. It seemed a little pushy, but it was Rattus, the gods of Finnish punk, after all. I thought about this for about five minutes and then said, "I can make this happen."

I explained to Vote that I could do a tour for them, but that it would have to start in Florida. I assured them that we'd make it to New York City, which they all wanted to see. I went back and forth with Vote and the members of Rattus by email for weeks polishing the details.

The guys in Rattus told me what kind of gear they wanted to play on. I was able to get most of their wants, but I could not secure a Rickenbacker bass. I found a support band who generously agreed to tour for nothing and provide their gear for Rattus. The support band was Reason of Insanity, from New Orleans. They were on my record label. They were a great band that I felt was extremely underrated. I thought this tour would do them some good. (And it did.)

I booked two weeks of shows on the east coast of the U.S. and promoted like crazy. It was Rattus' first trip to the U.S. Longtime fans had been waiting for this for, uh... a long time.

When the big day came, I picked up Rattus at the airport and took them back to my house where I showed them some of their equipment and went over the tour plans with them. Then we walked to a convenience store so they could buy cheap American beer. They sat up most of the night on my front porch talking and drinking. I stayed up with them for a while. It was guitarist/vocalist Jakke, his brother Tomppa, the bassist; Vellu, the drummer and, of course, manager Vote Vasko. Fortunately, their English was good and they were nice guys. That was important; we'd be spending two weeks together in a van.

About this time, Reason of Insanity pulled into town and went directly to the record store, where my employee Sam let them in for an all-night rehearsal in the storage room—and I imagine some drinking.

Sam was to be the roadie for the tour. Sam smoked cigarettes. I told him that he could not smoke in my van and that he had to quit smoking before the tour or I'd take someone else. Sam said he'd quit, no problem. He didn't quit, but the other person I had in mind could not make the tour, so Sam was in. Needless to say, with Sam in the van, we were taking numerous "bathroom breaks," so he could smoke.

The first show of the tour, the first Rattus show on U.S. soil, was in the storage room of my record shop. I hoped that they'd be good. As soon as Jakke hit the first guitar chord, jaws hit the floor and my concerns evaporated. They were phenomenal. It was like standing in front of a bomb blast—for 45 minutes. I knew the next two weeks would be intense.

There were a couple of shows with disappointing turnouts, but performance was never an issue. Both Rattus and Reason of Insanity crushed audiences every night. The show in Providence remains one of the best I have ever seen. It was one of those nights when everything was perfect, when audience and band were in total synch. And by the end of the tour, it was evident that we were all part of the same thing. Four guys from Finland and six Americans, all connected by something large, something intangible and without boundaries.

Finnish punk gods Rattus practicing unplugged in our living room.
Photo by Ella.

RAW POWER
SCREAMS FROM THE GUTTER LP
TOXIC SHOCK 1985

I'd first heard Italy's Raw Power around 1985 when a friend let me borrow the international punk compilation album, *Welcome to 1984*. Every band on that record is a destroyer and the album itself has been a huge eye opener for thousands, featuring bands from Sweden, Finland, Norway, Germany, Japan, and Australia.

The Raw Power track was one of the strongest with their histrionic, tonsil-shredding vocals and bizarre use of cowbell. I immediately put them on my mental checklist of bands to explore. Eventually I owned almost all of their records. In 1998, I got the chance to put on a gig for them.

Raw Power toured the states many times in the 1980s. They were one of the first, if not the first, non-UK punk bands to visit the U.S. They have seen more of the country than most Americans ever will. I missed my chance to see Raw Power open for the Dead Kennedys because I couldn't convince my mother to let me go to Miami on a school night. So 1998 was my chance to finally see these Italian leviathans.

They were supposed to play at a small venue in St. Petersburg, Florida. I wanted to get my band on the bill, so I called the club and the number was disconnected. They'd gone out of business. I found out about this two weeks before the scheduled date.

I knew the guy managing their tour, so I called to let him know that the club no longer existed. The club didn't bother to contact the band who would have shown up to locked doors. I asked the tour manager to let me move the show to another venue. For whatever reason, he took a week to give me his answer. By the time he said yes, I had seven days to secure a venue, find opening bands, and promote.

A teenager named Matt was working at a pizza parlor in Bloomingdale, a suburb of Tampa, and he'd talked the owner into letting bands play there sometimes. It was a great way for him to sell extra pizza and drinks. I asked Matt if he could get me a show for Raw Power, but he was no longer working there. So I contacted the owner.

I just walked in, requested to speak to the owner, and asked him if a band from Italy could play in his restaurant. He was excited that the band was from Italy. I think that is what won him over. In any case, he said yes almost instantly.

"They're really from Italy?" he asked me three times. Deal.

I made a kick ass flyer using one of the photos from the back of *Screams from the Gutter*, my favorite of their albums. I gave handfuls of flyers to the local bands and to every kid who walked into my record store. I also drove around town plastering flyers everywhere I could.

Raw Power was touring with an American band that was providing the equipment for the tour. The day before, both bands played in New Orleans, about ten hours away. To add a degree of difficulty, the band was fleeing New Orleans with a hurricane on their tail.

Hurricane George whipped into New Orleans hours after Raw Power's set, following them toward Florida. They kept ahead of the worst, but still had to fight lots of wind and rain, slowing their trip to almost fourteen hours. To further complicate things, the American band they were touring with broke down and could not finish the tour.

Mauro, the singer of Raw Power, called me from the road. He told me that they were still coming but they needed to borrow amps and drums. They only had their guitars with them. I told him that it would not be a problem. The local bands would be happy to share.

With a major hurricane coming our way, the weather was nasty the day of the show. People called me all day at the record shop to see if the show was still on. Yes, without a doubt. There was a rumor that it had been canceled. I was on bullshit control all day. I called people to remind them about the show and assure them that no act of nature could stop Raw Power. They all said they'd be there.

Mauro called me several times throughout the day to apprise me of their progress. He told me the weather was so bad they were driving just 40 miles per hour.

Finally Mauro phoned me to say that they were in town but he didn't know exactly where they were. I asked him to describe what he could see; he was calling me from about 500 feet away. I stepped outside of my record store with my cordless phone and waved to him and the rest of the band across the parking lot. They waved back and we walked to meet each other.

Mauro speaks perfect English. He went to college in London for eight years. He is highly educated and highly articulate. The other guys in the band spoke little English. Their Italian was excellent- I assumed. At least it sounded cool.

I showed Mauro and his brother Giuseppe, the guitarist, the flyer I made, using a photo from their 1985 album. They laughed and Mauro said, "We were just children then." I recall an interview with Raw Power in which Mauro said his motivation for keeping the band together was his brother. He said, "If I ever tried to quit, he'd kill me!"

We pulled into the parking lot of the pizza place and walked in to meet the owner. It was packed with people. Almost the entire crowd was high school students. There were maybe four or five older people there to see the show. Old Raw Power fans. As we were walking in, I overheard one of these older guys, a notorious cheapskate, ask the owner, "If Raw Power doesn't show up, do we get our money back?" The owner said no! Then the guy saw Raw Power walk in and forked over his money.

The owner was thrilled to have some real Italians in his restaurant. He shook all of their hands and told them that after the show he'd make a special pizza for them.

As the crowd paid their five dollars, a powerful hurricane barreled towards the small suburban pizza parlor. Some of the kids gawked at Raw Power. For many, it was their first concert and it was the first time they'd seen a band from Italy. In turn, the guys from Raw Power gawked at the pretty high school girls. Leered is more like it. They are Italian, after all. To their credit, I saw no ass pinching.

One or two local bands played and then it was Raw Power's turn. The opening bands were made up of high schoolers and their gear was less than pro—practice amps and a small, beat up drum kit. As the drummer sat down at the kit, he rolled his eyes, tossed up his hands and said what must have been Italian for, "I'm supposed to play this piece of shit?"

But once the band kicked in, any inadequacies in the equipment were easily overpowered by their sheer ferocity. It was an intense show. The dancing was spirited, but not violent. Friends were having a blast on a stormy night. During the

Raw Power at the Pizza Nook in Bloomingdale, FL.
Photo by Bob Suren.

song, "State Oppression," one amped-up teen grabbed my shirt by the shoulder and ripped out a huge chunk of fabric.

As promised, after the show the owner fired up the oven and made a special pizza the size of a mountain bike wheel for the band. They invited me to dig in with them. The owner stood by waiting for their approval. After a few bites, he said, "So, how's the pie?" The guys all gave him the thumbs up and he beamed with pride. He told them he never heard of their band but they were welcome back any time.

After the pizza, the band hopped into their tour vehicle and blasted off to the next gig in Miami, with Hurricane George following them all the way.

In 2002, Giuseppe had a heart attack while playing soccer and died. I contacted Mauro to tell him how sorry I was to hear about his brother. I was not sure if he knew who I was so I asked him if he remembered the show in the pizza parlor on the stormy night. Yes, he said. In fact they'd written the song "George" about it on their *Trust Me* album.

REASON OF INSANITY

S/T LP
PSYCHO WOLF RECORDS 2005

Harold Burkenstock, the singer of Reason of Insanity, is one of my favorite people. And not just in music, mind you. He's friendly, helpful, polite, and soft spoken almost to the point of shyness. I have literally heard him say, "Aw, shucks." He's that kind of guy. His real-life persona is quite different than what he throws down on stage and in the recording studio. In those situations, he's a wild animal.

I got to know Harold as a mail order customer. For several years, he and the few other punk rock guys in Lafayette, Louisiana sent envelope after envelope of well-concealed cash and money orders to my PO Box for records they could find nowhere else. I sent a lot of boxes over the years to his address on Honeysuckle Lane.

He often called on the phone to ask questions about music and just to talk. He is affable to the point of being a little goofy. It was hard not to like the guy, and we'd never even met. I was always busy when he called and usually had to be the one to end the conversation. He would apologize with a sincerity I have seen nowhere else. You may also add "earnest" to the list of his fine attributes.

Sometime in 1999 or 2000, Harold told me he started a band. I asked him to send a cassette. Almost everyone I talked to back then was in a band, but I rarely asked any of them to send tapes. I was buried in work all the time and just did not have the hours or motivation to check out demo tapes with the attention they deserved. Still, I was flooded weekly with cassettes. The listening pile grew to overwhelming stature and I grew to hate the sight of cassettes. Many of these tapes only got a quick play and were given away to friends. I probably missed a few gems.

But I wanted to hear Harold's band. He sent a tape full of forceful vocals and sinewy riffs. I asked him if he'd like to make a record. By his reaction, you'd think I told him he won the lottery or got to become a member of his favorite group. My record label was not that large, but to Harold it was a huge deal. As the years passed, I helped the band release three records, but their best effort was the self-titled album they produced on their own in 2005.

Nonetheless Harold always felt that my label, Burrito Records, was the band's true home. He got a massive tattoo on his left rib cage of a bandito with the words, "Burrito Hardcore" inscribed below. His body is covered with homages to his favorite bands, like Rattus, Poison Idea, Lipcream, and G.I.S.M. This music is Harold's lifestyle and not merely a choice of entertainment. I respect his level of dedication.

In 2004, Rattus needed an opening band for a two-week U.S. tour. Reason of Insanity was my first choice. The band was underappreciated. I thought that touring with a larger, more popular band would get them in front of some bigger crowds and build their fan base. Reason of Insanity was almost unknown but they delivered so hard every night that they blew away audiences in even the most jaded cities. After the tour, they had quite a buzz on the Internet. People wanted to know who they were. After five or six years with little notice, record sales picked up and they got offers from other labels.

Most nights of the tour found Harold on stage in his underpants and high tops, pouncing like a beast, breaking microphones and bottles and whatever else. It was all in good fun, never malicious. One night the cost of a broken microphone was taken out of our pay. Harold was overly apologetic. Hey, shit happens when you rock that hard, man.

Since Reason of Insanity was the support band and we were traveling on a shoestring, I was not able to pay them every night. The headlining band got first cut and after that, there was never much left. Harold didn't care. He was thrilled to be on the road with one of his favorite bands. When I did have a few bucks to toss their way, I had to force him to take the money.

Toward the end of the tour, it occurred to me that I had not seen Harold eat in a couple of days. We were at a highway rest area. I offered to buy him a sandwich and he refused.

"I'm not that hungry," he said. He looked hungry.

I was eating a bag of peanuts. I had half a bag left and offered it to him. He wouldn't take it. I asked a couple more times and finally he accepted the handful of peanuts.

He was literally working for peanuts. One of his band mates offered to buy him a meal and again he refused.

"Bob just gave me his peanuts. I'm fine." He thanked me again for the peanuts.

On the worst day of my life, Harold called me just to talk. He called while I was thinking about suicide. I love Harold, but I could not tell him what was wrong. I wasn't telling anyone yet. I was usually just stressed about money. That must have crossed his mind.

A week later I got an unexpected package in the mail from Harold. In the box was a bunch of records and a check for one hundred dollars. There was a letter saying that he didn't know what was bothering me, but he hoped this would help. He also thanked me again for all I'd done for the band. He invited me to come for a visit if that's what I needed. I called him right up to fill him in on my situation and to thank him for being such a good friend.

Punk rock's nicest guy, Harold Burkenstock,
March 2003 at Sound Idea. Photographer unknown.

RICHARD HELL AND THE VOIDOIDS
BLANK GENERATION LP
SIRE RECORDS 1977

I needed more records. In order to find more records, I hosted record meets. Make the records come to me. That was the plan. It always worked.

When the store was open, I held the meets there, in the storage room. It got crowded but it was fun. After the store closed, I started doing the meets in a picnic pavilion in a public park. I never got a permit for the pavilion. I just acted like I belonged there and no one challenged me. It was the punk rock approach.

Some of the meets in the park were goldmines; a few were slow. But I always found at least one or two things I didn't have, so it was always worth it. These were buy/sell/trade events. I encouraged trading. Attendance and vendor space were free. There was no reason not to go.

Sometimes people would ask me, "Is it going to be a good one? Should I come?" I hated these candy asses and their questions. I'm not psychic. I never had any way to tell how many people would show up or what they'd bring. My answer was a rhyme: "You won't know if you don't go." That rhyme holds true for a lot of things. Show up and find out.

In most cases, the best finds were right at the beginning. But sometimes a guy would show up with vinyl treasure in the last hour. People who arrived late or left early missed the gems.

One time a red-haired guy from Fort Lauderdale turned up with a cornucopia of really rare records. Nobody knew who the guy was. The records were so rare that nobody had anything good enough to offer in trade. And we were afraid to ask him for prices. Finally someone broke the ice. The guy was selling his records for about a third of what he should have been selling them for. In a few minutes, just about everything was gone. I got a couple of monsters from him. Either he didn't know their values or he didn't care. We never saw that guy again. You won't know if you don't go. Write that down.

Between 1995 and 2012, I put on 35 record meets. The first 34 were to build my collection. The last one was to deplete it. Not many people went to the last one. That's too bad because they missed some bargains.

Record swap at Sound Idea, 1996. Photo by Bob Suren.

SEX PISTOLS
NEVER MIND THE BOLLOCKS LP
EMI 1977

The Sex Pistols were a big band, a pivotal moment, for a lot of people. Not me. When I first heard the Pistols, I thought they were boring. I heard them well after the fact. I was born too late, as the Saint Vitus song goes.

I got into punk around 1983. *Never Mind the Bollocks* came out six years earlier. By the time a copy made it to my turntable, punk had given birth to its nasty offspring, hardcore. And that toddler was running all over the place, knocking things down, and getting uglier every day. The intensity of the genre built exponentially.

My heroes were miles ahead of the Pistols in terms of aggression. So that four-dollar second-hand copy of *Never Mind the Bollocks* did not have quite the impact it had for impressionable ears back in 1977. It reminded me of the Rolling Stones, who at the time I considered to be the very symbol of all that was tired and trite. (Hardcores could be quite dismissive.)

But I kept the record. Shelved it in a plastic bag and sneered whenever the Sex Pistols came up in conversation. (A lot of hardcores did that). "Sex Pistols" was somewhat of an insult at the time. Something you said to "poseurs." (Hardcores could be real dicks.)

Many years later when I knew more about music and when my palate had broadened a bit, I pulled out that old Sex Pistols album and it rocked me harder than I expected. The guitar tone is flawless. The delivery is sharper than a razorblade. The production is punchy. You can almost feel Johnny Rotten's spittle spattering in your eyes.

Glad I held onto that thing. It was a prime example of the arrogance of youth. Unfortunately, I did not hold onto my rare Crime singles. I'd acquired them dirt cheap, but at the time, I felt they were too slow. At the time, all I wanted to hear was thrash. And so, the Crime singles sold way too early (and cheaply) to a collector in Japan, who hopefully still has them and gives them the love they deserve. I dropped the ball with them, big time!

But this whole idea of hearing music way after the fact has me thinking. What will endure and what will seem pale ten, fifteen, or twenty years from now? I'd like to envision a future in which weird people still want to hear the Germs, Flipper, and the Ramones, but is it likely? Will today's fastest, craziest, most extreme bands seem like quaint relics to future listeners? I don't know. People still listen to the Rolling Stones, right?

SLAP OF REALITY
STUCK INSIDE 7"
VINYL COMMUNICATIONS 1989

When I think of Slap of Reality, I think of the series of events that took my life in a different direction than the one I had planned. I was in community college in Stuart, getting ready to move up to Gainesville to attend the University of Florida. I was studying journalism. I wanted to be a reporter. Finish college, get a job, marry my girlfriend, have kids. That was the plan. That was what normal people did, I assumed. I considered myself normal.

I saw a review for the first Slap of Reality record, the *Stuck Inside* 7", in *Maximum Rocknroll* and knew I needed it. I needed it because the reviewer mentioned that the band was from Florida. It was important to own every Florida punk record ever made, a goal I nearly accomplished.

So, I sent cash through the mail to an address in Chula Vista, California—to the label that put out the record—and a few weeks later a splendid green vinyl copy arrived in my mailbox. The title track was the stand out, but I played the record in its entirety many times. I think it was probably the best record I bought that year. Certainly it was the most impactful.

A year or so later, I was in Gainesville, studying journalism and scouring the four local record shops for gems every day after class. As I was walking down University Avenue one day on my way to the record shops, I sighted a Slap of Reality show bill stapled to a utility pole.

All of the utility poles in Gainesville were (and probably still are) covered in flyers for all kinds of things. How this one happed to catch my eye among the mosaic of handbills I don't know, but I am glad it did. Slap of Reality had a gig in Gainesville in just a few days, within walking distance of my dorm, at the famed Hardback Café, which was still a new thing.

I counted down the days until the show and when the date arrived, I made the solo walk to the Hardback with my trusty camera. I tried to shoot every band I saw.

At the show, I got upfront and shot a dozen pictures of the band. I realized that these guys were about my age, maybe a little younger, and that they handled themselves on stage professionally. They were a working band. I was impressed.

After the set, I approached the singer, Frank Lacatena, to tell him that I got some good shots and that I'd be happy to send him copies if he gave me his address. And he was kind of a jerk to me. He said, "I don't handle that stuff, talk to our drummer." Twenty-two years later I recounted this story while being filmed for a Tampa punk rock documentary. The filmmaker told Frank and he had no recollection of this, but still apologized to me. We're cool.

So, I went to talk to the drummer and that is how I met Rob Sexton, who became one of my best friends, band mate, and something of a mentor for a time.

Rob was sitting on the brick sidewalk in front of the Hardback with a semi-circle of people around him. They were talking about records. I awkwardly waited outside of the semi-circle until there was a gap in the conversation and then introduced myself. And he was cool to me.

Rob gave me his address and maybe a week later I sent him the photos. Shortly after that, Rob wrote me back saying that the photos were great and that they'd like to use the one of bassist Jon Ramos in their upcoming album if I would give them permission. Sure, of course. Rob promised to give me a photo credit, thank me in the album, and send me a free copy, all of which happened.

But more importantly, Rob and I continued corresponding by mail and sometimes by phone. Meanwhile, the girlfriend waiting for me back home cheated on me—twice—and then broke up with me—during final exam week of my last semester. Needless to say, I was a wreck for finals and graduation day sucked. All of the plans I made for after college were up in smoke. I returned to my hometown with a college degree and nothing else. I moved back in with my parents and got a nothing job.

Rob invited me to come visit him in Tampa so I did. It would be the first time I saw him since the gig in Gainesville. Rob had a huge record collection that he let me dig through. He told me about all kinds of bands that I never heard of. We went out to eat and to a show. Tampa seemed cool. I started visiting almost every weekend.

Eventually Rob and I began playing music together. I drove to Tampa every Saturday morning for three years for band practice, record shopping, shows, and Chinese food. I heard a lot of good music in his room. And the band we formed led me to meet lots of talented, sharp people who are still my friends. We toured the country a couple of times and made four records together. Great times.

One day while we were driving back from band practice, Rob said, "Why don't you just move here? You're here every weekend." It never occurred to me to move. It was an excellent idea. I had nothing in Stuart. Tampa was fun. Why not? Nobody in my immediate family ever left Stuart. It works for them; it was a bad fit for me.

Rob came up with the idea of opening a record store together. When it came down to it, Rob was not able to commit, so I did it on my own.

My family thought I was nuts to leave Stuart. My dad was not happy that I was opening a record store instead of using the college degree that he paid for. (He still sorely brings this up now and then.) My life didn't turn out the way I planned it at all. It turned out much more interesting.

Rob Sexton skips rope, April 1993. Photo by Bob Suren.

SORTO
AINA VALMIINA 7"
IKBALS RECORDS 1986

In the first two decades of punk, it seemed like everyone knew everyone, at least by reputation. It was a smaller world and a simpler world and it felt like punks were all on the same team. Not everyone was a saint, not everyone was friends, but there was a certain code of conduct that was unwritten but understood.

Over time, new generations entered the scene, old ones died out, and the code became diluted. I'm not trying to glorify "the good old days," but as the music scene grew larger, faster, and more convenient, it also became less personal. The original tenets have been left in the dust. The most basic of these tenets being, "Don't rip anyone off."

Over a course of 30 years in punk rock, as a fan and as a business owner, I have successfully completed tens of thousands of sales, purchases and trades through the mail. Rip offs were very rare. In all of that time, there are only four or five people who scammed me and got away with it.

Around 2002, it looked like a guy in Oregon was ripping me off for three rare records. I had done plenty of business with this guy over the years and it seemed out of character. We agreed to a trade by telephone. The next day, I sent the things he wanted. Weeks passed and I never got my stuff. I called him and got a promise that he would ship right away. More weeks passed and still no package.

Months passed. Now this guy was dodging my calls and not responding to emails. I was getting frustrated. Of course I wanted the three rare records for my collection, but what really singed me was that this was an older member of the music community. He knew better. He knew the code. My stomach burned with what I assumed to be an ulcer. I sat awake at night plotting revenge.

My wife, Ella, could tell that something was bothering me. I didn't go into all of the details, but I told her a guy was ripping me off and that I thought I might have to go beat his ass. To my surprise, she told me, "Yeah, you should." Ella is the most gentle, reasonable, diplomatic person you can imagine. And she seemed to be giving me consent for vengeance.

I knew the guy's home address. Someone was going to let me borrow a Domino's Pizza uniform. I got a map of the guy's town from the Internet and researched the area. I found what I needed. The plan came together nicely.

My idea was to get an early morning flight to Oregon and rent a car. First stop was to be at a gun shop a couple of miles from the guy's house where I planned to buy pepper spray and a stun gun. Next I'd go to a Domino's Pizza and buy a pizza. Then I would drive to the guy's house and stake it out, see what the neighbors were like, look at the surrounding streets, and wait until I saw the guy.

When I was sure the guy was home alone, I'd slip into the Domino's uniform, pocket the pepper spray and stun gun, grab the pizza, and head for the door. I was going to knock on the door and say, "Pizza guy!" He would be expecting no pizza. I would have the element of surprise.

When he opened the door, I was going to slam him in the face with the pizza, pepper spray his eyes and then zap him with the stun gun until he passed out. I planned to bring some duct tape from home to bind and gag him, too.

After this fucker was bound, gagged, and beaten unconscious, I planned to grab his entire record collection, drive it to a UPS place and ship it back home to me. Then I'd have a couple of hours to kill until my red-eye flight back to Tampa. What could go wrong? It was the perfect plan, right? I thought so.

I went over the plan for a few days. There were a few risks, but I was willing to take them—all for three records. It seems trivial now, but at the time, I was consumed with thoughts of revenge. Keep in mind, these were very rare records.

When I was satisfied with my plan, there was one more thing to do: Clear it with the wife. I probably should have done that before I bought the plane tickets, but I didn't.

I called sweet, patient, supportive Ella at home and told her, "Well, I fly to Oregon on Tuesday morning and I'll be back Tuesday night." She had no idea what I was talking about.

I reminded her about the guy in Oregon who was ripping me off and gave her a skeletonized version of my plan. She became extremely upset.

"I didn't think you were serious about that. I have to go now. I think I'm going to be sick." She did get sick. When I got home from the record shop that night, she told me that my plan made her vomit and that if I ever thought about doing anything like that again she would have to divorce me. I canceled my plane tickets. I needed a better plan.

As much as I hated the idea, it seemed like I would have to involve the authorities to get my three records. I called the police in Oregon, assuming they'd just laugh at me, but the officer I got on the line was very concerned. He took some information from me and after considering it for a while said, "If you are in another state, and this involves the mail, it is a federal crime. I'm turning this over to the FBI."

I figured that was the last I'd hear of it, but less than an hour later, an FBI agent called me at the record shop and asked me for the full story. He, too, was very concerned. He asked me to verify the guy's address and asked me about the value of the three records.

"Well, no doubt about it, this is a felony on the federal level. I'm going there now to investigate."

I couldn't believe the FBI was getting involved in a record trade gone wrong, but this hard-ass was on the case. Thirty minutes later, he called me from the guy's house with his report.

"I am here now. I have seen the records. Mr. M. is packing them up right now in front of me. He promised me he would mail them tomorrow. If you do not have them in one week, I want you to call me so I can follow up." Holy shit!

The agent gave me his number at the FBI and his personal phone number. He wanted me to call him when the records arrived. A few days later, I got the records, called the agent, and thanked him for his help.

STALIN
GO GO STALIN 12"
CLIMAX RECORDS 1983

I always tried to make people feel welcome at my record store. If they were sincerely into the music, they were my allies and I wanted to keep them around. There were also a few people who rubbed me wrong who I hoped would disappear, but these people were rare. For the most part, I wanted to see a large, unified crowd. Given human dynamics, this was not completely possible but I did the best I could.

Every once in a while some awkward, young person would amble into the place, clearly looking for something to be part of. I remembered how a few people welcomed me into the scene when I was a nascent punk rocker. It was my turn to do the welcoming. I would introduce these fledglings to people, invite them to the Saturday night concerts in the storage room and generally try to help them feel comfortable. Usually it worked.

There was one awkward, young person I really liked. He was painfully shy and stuttered a little. I copied lots of music for him and invited him to all of the concerts. He usually came alone. I tried introducing him to a few people, but nobody made a connection. I didn't understand it. He was nice. The people I introduced him to were nice but it didn't click.

Punk rock is supposed to be democratic. Everybody counts. Everybody can contribute something. There is not supposed to be division between band and audience. But in some places you'll find an elitist, country club mentality. Even back in the "golden years" of the early 80s, there were punk snobs.

I recall going to an excellent record store with a few friends when I was in high school. I couldn't wait to finally check it out. Unfortunately, it was inhabited by punk rock snobs.

This place stocked the most obscure punk rock titles from around the world at a time when very few people were interested in such things. It was a niche within a niche. The selection was so esoteric that I still have no idea how they remained in business. There were records from Germany, Italy, Finland, Sweden, and Yugoslavia.

One of the records I saw that day was a 12" by the Stalin from Japan. I think this is the first Japanese record I ever saw. It had Japanese characters on the cover and just looked so cool. Then I noticed the name of the band. The Stalin? That's terrible! Why would anyone name a band after Josef Stalin? That was almost as bad as naming your band after Hitler. I didn't pick it up.

I kept looking while the cool people hanging out in the shop watched me and my less-punk-looking friends. They were whispering something.

All of the records looked interesting, but I didn't know what anything was. I was out of my element in a punk rock record store. Finally I saw a record by a band I recognized. It was an album by Black Flag, a popular and important American band. It might have been the only American record in the whole place. The gourmet punks were still watching us and making comments. When I picked up the Black Flag record, they laughed. Black Flag was too mundane for them. What a bunch of jerks.

I left without buying anything. I should have bought the Stalin record or something equally arcane. But we just wanted to get out of there. We never went back.

Ten years later, I purchased a large record collection. One of the items was a Stalin 12". I asked the guy where he found it. He got it at the store I'd visited a decade earlier. It may very well have been the exact copy I saw that day.

In 2012 when I sold my collection, the awkward, young person who I really liked, the one nobody else warmed up to, he got the Stalin record.

TELEVISION
MARQUEE MOON LP
ELEKTRA RECORDS 1977

Ella and I enjoyed walking the neighborhood after dark. We liked looking at houses and getting ideas for our own. We liked landscaping. I enjoyed owning a house with Ella and making little improvements. It felt like we were heading in the right direction.

These walks were special. They made me feel close to her. Sometimes we held hands. I love holding hands. I love marriage.

Ella could not always go for the walks. Sometimes she had too much work or she was too tired. She started saying no more often. I started going for walks on my own. My solo walks were usually longer than our together walks. I brought my iPod with me.

I love my iPod. I bought the one with the most memory. For a guy who was always broke, it was a major investment worth every penny. I have used it every day for years without a problem. I relish having thousands of records on a thing the size of a deck of cards. I can listen to anything I want, whenever I want. The portability and convenience are difficult to ignore. No wonder the music industry took such a hit.

Television was my solo walking music. It's the right tempo and the right timbre. Mood music. On headphones, I can pick up every nuance. That record always surprises me with its subtle brilliance.

TERRORAIN
1988 DEMOS 7"
BURRITO RECORDS 2000

By 1995, I was running a record label, a record store, a wholesale distributorship and a mail order operation, all out of 113-H East Brandon Blvd. All of these were tightly linked. They supported each other. The mail order part of the business was the most profitable. It was the cornerstone. Without it, the other pieces would have collapsed.

I liked doing the mail order. What I enjoyed most was getting to know the repeat customers. We had a lot of interesting ones, like the guy who groomed Pamela Andersonís dogs and the guy who worked at the Museum of Modern Art in New York. Punk rock brings together all types.

I had a toll free number so customers could call, ask questions and pay by credit card. One of our favorite repeat customers was an affable Brit named Patrick Lawlor. The company Patrick worked for had stationed him in Arizona for a couple of years. His wife was home in England. He got to visit her every few months, but I imagine that Patrick got lonely and bored in Arizona because he started calling my toll free number all the time.

At first these calls were strictly business, but with frequency they became more social. All of us at 113-H enjoyed it when Patrick called. He was always good for a laugh and over time he revealed more of his personality. He also has an incredible knowledge of music, which he unveiled with amazing stories about European bands we in the States never got to see.

Patrick told me his introduction to punk was hearing the primeval UK band the Adverts performing a song called, ìGary Gilmoreís Eyesî on Radio Luxembourg back in 1977 when he was just a bored teenager. And like that, Patrick was hooked for life. He saw the Sex Pistols, the Clash, Discharge, Crass, and every important European band you can name.

He told us stories about seeing seminal American bands like Crucifix and the Bad Brains play their first UK dates. He said the Bad Brains played so fast that the UK punks didnít know how to react. One confused Brit punk asked them to play a slow song so he could dance without getting his hair messed up!

Patrick and a friend followed Californiaís mighty Black Flag to every show on every one of their UK tours. (Decades later, he named his son ìHenryî after Black Flag singer Henry Rollins.) Patrick is living history, a walking encyclopediaóand a really nice guy.

One day in the summer of 2000, he called to order a pile of records. After I totaled him up and charged his card, the chit chat started up as usual. He casually mentioned that he had been in a band called Terrorain for a few months in 1988. I said I never heard of the band and he was not surprised. They only played a few shows before splitting up.

I asked if Terrorain ever recorded anything. He said they recorded a demo tape. He downplayed this, saying that it was not that great. I told him Iíd like to hear it. I had a feeling it would kick ass.

A little while later, Patrick sent me his personal copy of the Terrorain demo tape and it did kick ass. I told him Iíd like to make it into a record. He was surprised.

ìReally? Nobody knows who we were. Weíve been broken up twelve years!î

I told him I liked the music and I was willing to take a chance. That was how I ran the label. I just put out stuff that I liked. I never could gauge how something would sell. But my gut told me that Terrorain was great and that enough people would pick up on it that I wouldnít lose money.

I asked Patrick to send me whatever graphics he might have so I could put together the packaging. He sent me a sticker and the few existing photos of the band. They were not around long enough to have accrued much in the way of memorabilia. But what he sent me was enough.

I took the original cassette tape to a great recording studio and worked with a great engineer to make the music sound stronger than ever. Several weeks later, the record was finished. It became one of the most popular titles on my label. Patrick was so happy that he wanted to visit me in Florida. We met for the first time on Halloween 2000.

Patrick and his wife Julie stayed in the area for a few days. In that time we had dinner together and caught a concert. But most importantly, I conducted a long interview with him for a magazine in which he divulged priceless nuggets of insight and fascinating stories about his years in the UK music scene.

I have interviewed lots of people, but he was by far the best. We had chemistry. I asked good questions and he dug deep for earnest answers. Over the last fifteen years, I have transferred this interview to four new computers. It is still a great read.

In 2003, I wanted to do a two-day music festival with all of the bands on my record label. Almost all of them could do it. Patrick wanted to do a Terrorain set at the festival, but the other members of the band couldnít do it. My employee Sam said he could play the bass parts. We enlisted the drummer and guitarist of another band on the label, Reason of Insanity, to do the rest. These guys are pro musicians. I knew they could do it.

The day before the festival, Patrick flew into Tampa and met the American version of Terrorain for the first time. They stayed up all night practicing in the back of the record shop. Patrick blew out his voice practicing, but by show time, he was fine. The American Terrorain with Patrick on vocals killed. The crowd loved them. They ended up playing sets on both days of the festival. It was two days of intense music and good times. New friendships were made that weekend and old ones were bolstered.

This experience renewed Patrickís interest in playing music. He started a new band called War/System. In March 2008, he brought the new band to Florida for three gigs. After the third gig, he invited my band to tour the UK with War/System. The offer was too good to turn down, so in November 2008, we jetted to England for gigs in Nottingham, Bristol, London, and Birmingham with our new friends in War/System.

And that was the last time I saw Patrick. I don't know if or when we'll cross paths again. I've talked to him on the phone hundreds of times but we've only seen each other in person on four occasions. And even though we've only had a dozen days together, he's one of my best friends.

Me and Pat Lawlor at the Meathouse, March 2006, Tampa, FL. Photographer unknown.

TOXIC REASONS
KILL BY REMOTE CONTROL LP
SIXTH INTERNATIONAL RECORDS 1984

Many people prefer the first Toxic Reasons album, *Independence,* to the second, *Kill by Remote Control.* Both are excellent albums, but I heard *Kill* first and many more times, so it has a special place in my heart. It was one of the first full-length punk albums I ever heard, on loan from a friend, and one of the first I sought out for purchase.

It was several years before I was even aware of *Independence.* Information was harder to come by back then; the conduit was magazines and friends. None of us had *Independence,* so to us it did not exist. Funny, there are a lot of important punk records that never made it to our circle that I had to pick up on a decade late to the party. But the ones that did reach us had the power to sculpt our views, our tastes, our opinions. I feel lucky to have found *Kill by Remote Control* while it was still fresh.

Two years later, I found a flyer for a show with Toxic Reasons and the Bad Brains at the Cameo Theatre in Miami. I showed it to one of my friends and asked, "Wow, who's going to headline?"

His response was curt: "Who do you think?"

I honestly did not know. Of course, the Bad Brains headlined. They were a much larger band and are much better known today—Toxic Reasons' legacy is not as bright as it should be—but to me, Toxic Reasons were one of the biggest bands in the world. Or they should have been.

The song "Destroyer" was the immediate stand out. It still wows me. Around 2006, I ran into bassist David "Tufty" Clough at a bar and assaulted him with questions about the band. He was generous with his time but must have thought I was sort of a loon, particularly when I produced a UK pressing of *Kill by Remote Control* from my handbag and asked him about the two additional songs and alternate cover art. I had bought the album a little earlier in the evening from a friend, but Tufty must have thought I just walked around with it all the time in case I ran into him! The stunned look on his face when I pulled it out was classic.

Shortly after first hearing *Kill by Remote Control,* I saw the outstanding live footage of Toxic Reasons released by

Target Video. The live impact was even greater than the vinyl impact.

Bootleg copies of all the Target Video and Flipside Video titles circulated throughout our scene. These videos were my first exposure to a lot of my favorite bands and as close as I ever got to seeing some of them. I deemed these videos as important as *Maximum Rocknroll* or any record label. I grabbed as many dubs as I could.

After college I found myself back in my hometown, working at a small independent television station. I was promised a job as a news writer and possibly as an anchorman when the station grew a little and developed a news department. In the meanwhile, I was given a job as the master control operator. My duties were getting all of the programs and commercials on the air at the right time plus monitoring and adjusting the sound and picture quality. Basically, anything that went out over the air was my responsibility.

I stayed at the station for two years and there was never any sign of a news department on the horizon. I was stuck in the small master control room, which was fine for the most part. I got to read a lot of books and watch foreign television on satellite. Canada has some remarkable sitcoms.

But I got bored. And boredom turns my mind to mischief. Our station played a lot of infomercials late at night for gadgets and *Greatest Hits of the 70s* type-albums and a bunch of crap that nobody cared about. The owner of the station had no idea what was supposed to be on the air. He didn't even know half of our programs. Part of my job was to know the program schedule by heart. I also had a key to the station.

One Saturday night, I slipped into the station with a stack of video tapes and at the stroke of midnight, just as an infomercial for the Flow-Be was to air, I slipped in a Target Video compilation. That night I played the Lewd, Sick Pleasure, Black Flag, Code of Honor, and my heroes from Ohio, Toxic Reasons.

If anybody noticed the schedule change, I don't know. Nobody said anything to me. The next week, I tried it again. This time the station got a few phone calls. Nobody was supposed to be in the station at that hour, so I had to let the phone ring. If it was my boss calling and I picked up, I'd be busted.

The next week, I played a high quality Dead Kennedys video and the phone rang off the hook. And this time, people were leaving messages—not all of them positive. One caller threatened to burn down the station.

No big deal, I figured, I'll just erase the tape before I go. But when I went to erase the tape, I couldn't figure out how to do it. I started to worry. The tape would not erase! But I did figure out how to rewind the tape, so I hauled ass home and called the station myself. In my best redneck accent, I left a 30-minute message on the answering machine about how much I loved a fishing show. I just kept blabbering away, praising the stupid show until the answering machine cut off. When I returned to work on Monday morning, my boss was listening to the long message. He was about half way through my rant— and taking notes about what the caller liked so much.

He turned to me and said, "This guy sounds like a nut but he really likes the fishing show. I wish he left a phone number." I almost pissed myself.

My pirate television show seemed unstoppable. I got bolder with my choices, played longer videos, and sometimes brought friends to the station. And then on Monday morning, it was all business.

One Monday morning, my co-worker Tim the camera man approached me in the master control room and said, "I've been enjoying your show."

Tim and I were down. He was almost twice my age, but totally cool. He promised to keep it a secret. In fact, he wanted to know more about punk. He asked me to make him some tapes. I did that. He didn't like the music but was intrigued by the ideas and the subculture. I loaned him books and magazines which he devoured. He became the biggest fan of my TV show.

A few weeks after Tim stone-cold busted me, he came up to me by the coffee machine and asked, "Have you ever heard of the Genitorturers?" Yes, I had. I used to correspond with singer Jennifer Zimmerman when she was a college DJ in Orlando. We exchanged a lot of letters back then.

Tim told me that the Genitorturers were playing in Miami soon and that he wanted to go. Was I up for a road trip? Sure! Furthermore, Tim wanted to videotape the band. He asked me if I could put him in touch with Jennifer for permission. I did so and Jennifer kindly granted permission.

So, my friend Kate, Tim, and I, along with a $20,000 television camera made the trek to Miami in my Dodge Diplomat, a former police car. The Genitorturers were a glorious spectacle. Tim got great video that we never did anything with, but it was cool to watch.

I continued hosting my anonymous punk rock video show, every Saturday at midnight. Tim would critique my shows on Monday mornings, telling me if my transitions were smooth and what video was good quality and what stuff was too rough to watch. At one point he suggested coming clean to the boss and seeing if we could make it a legit show with him as producer. But after further thought, we realized that this was a bad idea and not as much fun. The Target Videos continued to play a critical role in my programming. They were the main course.

At the 2011 Sarasota Film Festival, Target Video founder and visionary Joe Rees played three nights of classic and never-seen Target footage, including that arresting Toxic Reasons clip. After the third screening, I knew I had to meet him and tell him how important his videos were to me and to small town punks everywhere, to the people who never got to see the legends of his videos. I had to tell him about the big footsteps he left on so many brains. I actually got a little choked up trying to articulate this to him. I must have looked a little crazy.

Eventually I was able to compose myself and I told him about my misadventures at the TV station. He was positively enthralled. He had more questions for me than I had for him: "Where was this? When? How many people do you think saw it?" He was really tickled pink.

"Hold on, I have to get someone," he said. Joe ran off and came back with a woman who was his wife or his girlfriend or something and he made me retell the story. He was grinning the whole time. She thought it was great, too. I really made his night, I guess. Joe seemed completely unaware of what an effect his videos have had worldwide. Modest guy.

Several years earlier, when I was running my record store in small, safe Brandon, Florida, I made a mix tape which I dubbed and passed out to anyone who seemed to need a little schooling. It was an aural primer, a mix of all the big names and a few obscurities as food for thought. I probably made at least a hundred copies of that tape over the years. The very first song on it was "Destroyer."

VARAUS
1/2 LP
RAUS RECORDS 1983

As years ticked away, my collection grew fatter and fatter. I had all of the easy-to-find stuff. My predilections turned toward more exotic fare. Rare records, especially ones from foreign countries, made me drool. My want list was dense with Japanese, Swedish, Danish, Italian, Brazilian, Australian, Spanish, and Norwegian obscurities. I had a particular sweet tooth for Finnish music.

One of the rarest Finnish records is the Varaus 1/2 LP, so called because there is only music on one side. The other side is blank. It is half an album. I think only 300 copies were made, a long time ago in a country far, far away. Try finding one these days for less than a grand.

I found one in 1996. A guy I vaguely knew in Australia was selling his whole collection. He sent me a list, packed with foreign punk rock masterpieces. I didn't know what a lot of the stuff was but the prices were good and I was willing to take a chance. He was selling his Varaus record for twenty five dollars. Even back then, I knew that was a bargain.

The thing is, this guy had a reputation for being a rip off. People sent him money, it was said, and he never sent their stuff. Word travels fast in the punk rock grapevine, especially bad words.

I, on the other hand, had a reputation for honesty. I also had a reputation for being a hot head. Once, a guy in Scotland tried to rip me off for 200 records. Almost two years had passed without my records and he had stopped answering my letters—(he had no email address). I wrote him a letter saying that I would be in Scotland soon and that I planned to nail him to the floor by his cock and set his house on fire. I got my records a few weeks later. Feel free to use that line if you want.

Another time a guy from Poland visited me at the record shop. We talked about mutual friends in Poland. When I mentioned one guy, he told me that he was a total rip off. Really? That surprised me. I told him that I did business with the guy dozens of times without a hint of problem.

"That's because everyone in Poland is afraid of you."

He was completely serious.

I laughed out loud. I liked the idea of everyone in Poland being afraid of me. Sometimes a bad reputation can be a good thing. I was a hot head. I did send some nasty letters and emails over the years, but I never had to resort to real violence. The threats were enough.

Maybe that's why the guy in Australia was so accommodating. This was before electronic payments existed. International money orders were a pain in the ass. The guy asked me to send well-concealed cash through the mail. I was hesitant, but I wanted to get my hands on some rare records. I sent hundreds of dollars across the world, hidden in a CD case. He got it and I got my records.

I was stoked. I made two more purchases from him, well-concealed cash through the mail. I got all my records. They were all good and in good condition.

I got everything on his list that piqued my interest. A couple of weeks after my last box arrived, he was talking to someone on the phone, had a brain aneurysm and died. Bet you didn't see that one coming.

VKTMS
MIDGET 7"
EMERGENCY ROOM RECORDS 1979

It took me nearly twenty years to find the first VKTMS record. And when I got it, I didn't care.

I'd heard the incredible title track somewhere and was mesmerized by the tough girl vocals and hilarious lyrics, the title track being the greatest (and perhaps the only) song about midget cunnilingus ever written. I knew I needed that record and for many years, it remained at the top of my want list. A few copies slipped by me because I was either too broke or too cheap to pay the going rate. But in April of 2012, I arranged a trade with a fellow collector buddy in Canada.

I love trading. Get rid of something you have doubles of or no longer care about and get something great in return. No cash changes hands and both parties are happy. I waited patiently by my mailbox for a couple of weeks. Soon this coveted vinyl would be on my turntable.

Then on May 4, 2012, just weeks after our tenth anniversary, my entire life changed. Ella, my beautiful wife, my best friend and partner of seventeen years told me that she no longer loved me and wanted to separate. It was unbelievable news. I thought we were doing fine. I thought she was happy. I was shocked. The pain was agonizing. The next day, the fucking record arrived and I could not care less.

What was a coveted item was suddenly just a fucking thing. One of thousands of fucking things sitting in alphabetized rows in my living room. None of these things I spent my life hunting seemed important anymore. The archive that I'd put so much time and money into suddenly seemed to be a monument to minutiae. I felt I had wasted my years. I had ignored my lovely wife for the endless pursuit that is record collecting. I spent too much time on my own interests and not enough time being a husband. I felt like an idiot. I spent most of May 5 planning my own death.

It seemed like the right thing to do. It felt like my only option. I picked the date July 28, 2012 to kill myself with a gunshot to the chest in a public park near a river. I thought of all the things I would have to do, all the loose ends I would need to tie up before my suicide. Some of them were simple, like buying a gun and canceling my cell phone. Others were tough and would take time. I made a task schedule with July 28 as my literal deadline.

The biggest challenge was getting rid of my record collection. It was worth a small fortune and I knew that if I died, it would be left to waste. My wife wouldn't know what to do with it. I would sell it and leave her the money. Fucking money was always a stressor for us. I could finally do something about that.

On May 20, I began selling the records. They went in huge chunks, thousands of dollars at a time. When I told her I was going to sell my records, she knew something was wrong. She started crying and left the house for two days. When she returned, we held each other in tears.

July 28 was quickly approaching and I still had thousands of records left. This was going to take longer than I thought. Still, I kept plugging away, selling them any way I could. Meanwhile I was talking to my friends who offered me lots of love, support, and good advice.

Maybe I didn't need to destroy myself. Maybe I could get through this. I decided I would still sell my record collection and use the money to give her financial comfort and to help me start a new life. Beautiful Ella deserves every penny of the many thousands I have given her. She is the best person I have ever known. And I planned for my own future alone. The aforementioned task schedule remains on my computer as a file named JUL28. It is an organizational masterpiece, but one I will never implement. Why I keep it, I can't say.

While I still love all of this music, it is no longer important for me to be its curator. I have made digital copies of everything I'll ever want to listen to. The original artifacts are important, but I no longer feel the need to be their possessor. I am happy knowing that pieces of my collection have been scattered to good homes around the world. I don't miss any of them. The first VKTMS record is the last record I'll ever own.

I moved into 203 when Ella and I separated. It is less than a mile from the home we purchased together twelve years earlier. I wanted to be able to see her and our dogs once in a while. I didn't want to be too far away if she ever wanted me to come home. So many nights I lay awake hoping for that phone call. I imagined myself running all the way home.

203 is a small apartment, but quiet and clean. I could not have found a better place to live for my budget. The day Ella told me she no longer loved me I had twelve dollars to my name. I was 43 years old. What had I done with my years? I felt like I really fucked up. Forty-three and separated with twelve dollars to start over.

But I had a world-class record collection, which no longer seemed important. Without Ella in my life, these vinyl documents, these relics of my last 30 years, seemed trivial. The collection was worth a lot of money, around six figures by my guess. It was time to sell.

I know a collector who says—without a trace of humor—that he wants to be buried with his records, like some Egyptian royal. I've never wanted to be entombed in vinyl, but I never thought I'd sell a single thing. I thought of my collection as a giant collage or a puzzle with each piece being vital to the whole. I figured I'd keep it all forever or perhaps pass it on to someone special or maybe donate it to a library. But it was obvious what I had to do.

Before I moved out, I started selling the collection. In a matter of days, I had tens of thousands of dollars and I still had thousands of records yet to sell. I gave Ella wads of money, which she at first refused. She deserved it; I insisted. After I gave her what I could, I began apartment hunting.

The first place I looked at was nice but out of my price range. The landlord told me had another place I could check out. He gave me the address. I went by to look at it and felt like crying. It was a wreck. It was the saddest, crappiest apartment I have ever seen. I would not let a dog live there. A rat perhaps, but not a dog. That's all I can afford on my budget? Damn. This new life was going to be sadder than I thought.

On the same street, a couple of blocks away, a "For Rent" sign caught my eye. I pulled over and checked the place out. It was nice, which meant it was probably way out of my budget. But I called the number on the sign and later that day the landlord let me in.

The inside was nice, too. Simple but clean, cool and quiet. She told me the price. It was more than I wanted to pay, but I had a large cash reserve from selling records. I remembered the deal I made with the landlord at 113-H back in 1995. I thought that trick might work again.

I offered her a year's rent paid cash in full, on the spot, if she would knock two hundred dollars off the monthly rent. Like the landlord at 113-H, she was taken aback. She wanted to think about it.

The next day she called me and said she'd meet me in the middle. She gave me a one hundred dollars per month discount if I paid cash in full for the year. Deal. I met her at the apartment, handed her an envelope fattened with hundred dollar bills and signed the lease. I could move in the next day.

I told Ella about the deal I made and she was happy for me. She wanted to be around to see me off. She must have thought this would give us closure. I think it may have made things more painful. Packing my belongings while my wife watched me from the couch was one of the worst experiences of my life.

"Do I really have to do this?" I pleaded.

"Yes."

"Please, no."

"I'm sorry."

The sound of my shoes dropping into a cardboard box is the saddest thing I have ever heard. Six lonely thunks.

I packed my clothes, my computer, and my books. I asked if I could take a towel. She told me to take as many I as needed. I took only one. She told me to take some kitchen stuff. I took one dish, a fork, a knife and a spoon. She told me to take more, but I wouldn't.

I grabbed an old air mattress that we used for company. We had four or five air mattresses. Bands were always crashing at our house. Ella never seemed to mind these house guests. Some of them were fun.

And that was my first load. I drove the nine-tenths of a mile to 203 and dropped everything off. Then I went back for my records. As I started working on the records, I fell apart. It was all too real.

"Why did you want to be here for this?" I asked with a weird, high-pitched quaver in my voice that didn't sound like me.

"I thought it would be easier for you. I'm sorry."

We hugged and cried, me doing most of the crying.

"This is fucking awful. This is a nightmare. Please, no."

"I'm sorry."

It took me three van loads to move the records to 203. In a couple of hours I was moved in. I looked at the pieces of my life scattered all over the small, clean apartment and felt pathetic. My life in boxes. I blew up the air mattress and tried to sleep. There was nothing else to do.

That night I called a couple of people from the air mattress and told them my shitty story. I told it over and over to anyone who would listen. Nobody said anything that helped. They tried, but at that point, nothing got through. It was like putting a Band-Aid on a gunshot wound.

I slept on the air mattress for a few weeks. I figured sooner or later Ella would miss me and call me back home. She did miss me, she said. She missed my company and my jokes and my voice, but she couldn't call me home. She didn't love me anymore. She was certain we couldn't be together again. I know it was hard on her, too.

The air mattress was hard to sleep on. It moved around and it hurt my hips if I slept on one side too long. It looked like I would be at 203 for a while, so I went out and bought a bed. Buying a bed alone has got to be one of the most depressing things you can do. I remember thirteen years earlier shopping for beds with Ella and how happy we were when we found the right one. So many nice moments in that bed.

One night there was a heavy downpour and 203 flooded in a matter of minutes. I had almost no furniture. Everything I owned was on the floor, including my valuable record collection. I rushed around the apartment, picking up boxes and setting them on the kitchen counters, the stove, my folding-table desk and my new bed.

Fortunately, I was there at the time or things could have been much worse. Of the thousands of records I still had, maybe thirty or forty got wet. A few were pretty rare pieces, but luckily, most were more common items. I set them out to dry. Most of my books were ruined and had to be thrown out.

I called my landlord. She said she'd get there soon to check it out. There was two inches of water in every room of the apartment. I called Ella to ask for some help. She came right over with a wet vacuum and a few towels. Together we cleaned up much of the mess but it was clear I couldn't spend the night at the apartment. I asked her if I could stay at the house that night. Yes, she said, on the couch.

That night I stayed on the couch, crying and moaning, while the woman I loved slept a room away in our big bed. It was a terrible night. In the morning, I returned to 203.

Not much good ever happened at 203. I was in therapy. Therapy helped quite a bit, but at the end of the day, there I was, alone in my new bed while my wife slept alone less than a mile away. The nights were crushing.

Dr. R. encouraged me to keep moving and stay busy. He was right. I made an effort to get out of the house as much as possible and try new things. I wanted to meet new people.

Ella's birthday was coming up. I wondered how I should handle it. I got her a thoughtful present. She accepted it, but I don't know if she's ever used it. And I invited her out to lunch. She would not have lunch with me. I asked her three times; she politely but firmly declined.

The afternoon of Ella's birthday, I was invited to a barbeque at a friend's house. I was happy to have something to do that day. For once, I was good with mingling. There were a lot of people I knew there but a few strangers, too. I talked to everyone and made a couple of new friends.

The only moment I happened to be alone, something awesome happened. I was sitting in a chair, drinking a bottle of water, when a car pulled up to the party. An arresting blonde with long legs got out of the car. She walked directly over to me, sat down, and introduced herself. Her name was June.

She knew most of the people at the party. She'd never seen me before and yet she took a direct path to me and started a conversation. My heart stuttered. Her beauty was the hook, I admit, but the longer we talked, the more I liked her. She was funny, articulate, whimsical, and bright. And she had another quality that I still cannot define that was, and still is, irresistible to me. She is spellbinding. Like Ella, she has blue eyes that demand attention. I was completely smitten.

We passed an hour or more getting acquainted. We exchanged phone numbers and discussed getting together sometime. Then I had to rush off to band practice. It was the only time in my life that I did not want to be at band practice. I should have canceled but I couldn't.

I asked a few people about June. They told me that she's a wild card. Unpredictable. She seemed balanced, grounded, and well-spoken. They said she parties hard. I don't drink at all and I have never cared for drugs. On that basis, we seemed like a mismatch, but something about her that I still can't figure out is so enchanting that I wanted to try.

The party gave me an idea: Have a party! Yes, I would have my own party and invite June. I wanted something good to finally happen at 203. I picked out a date and asked June if she'd come. She said yes right away. Then I invited everyone else and started planning.

I spent hundreds of dollars on lawn furniture, grills, cooking utensils, food, and beverages. I don't eat meat, but I bought a bunch of meat. I don't drink beer, but I bought a bunch of beer. June likes beer. The whole party was so I could get closer to June. She didn't show up.

She didn't show up but it was a nice party. Finally, something good happened at 203. I felt better. I felt like life had possibilities where before I had only seen darkness and impending suicide.

The next week in therapy, I told Dr. R. about the party and June. He asked me if I thought she was a good companion for me. That was his way of saying that she probably was not. I saw his point, but I was so taken with her. I still am. For months I tossed and turned in bed hoping to be with Ella again. When she made it apparent that would never happen, I found myself wondering what it would be like to be with June. These two blue-eyed wonders bedeviled my sleep. They took turns keeping me awake.

Something else good happened at 203. Five months after the party, a strange twist brought June to my apartment. Nothing happened, but it was amazing that she was there. It was like a dream seeing her in the place where I thought of her so many times. She needed a ride somewhere and before we left, she needed to use my bathroom. While she was in the bathroom, I wrote a poem on a small piece of paper:

My hands are hungry to have you.
I want to be enveloped in whatever magic it is that makes you glow like you do.
You are tantalizing.
You delight me.
I want to dance with you in the most intimate way.
Please give yourself to me.
We'll devour each other.
I'll handle you like silk.
You'll feel like you are flying.

I looked at it for a second and wondered if I should give it to her. I quickly copied the poem to my computer. I folded the original and stuffed it in my pocket just as she came out of the bathroom. Later as I was driving her home, I handed her the folded paper and told her to read it when she was alone. She read it but she said it wasn't going to happen. I continued to sleep alone at 203.

Mailbox at 203 , May 2013.
Photo by Bob Suren.

WHERE: UNIT 49-B

After college, I learned how to screen print T-shirts. I wanted shirts of my favorite bands and I couldn't find them anywhere. I was a hungry fan.

I made one-of-a-kind shirts for myself. Whenever I wore them to concerts, I got lots of comments and questions. Some people asked me to make shirts for them. I usually said no, but eventually a few friends talked me into making a shirt or two now and then. I gave them away, traded them for records, or sold them cheaply. My intention with screen printing was not to make money. I just wanted cool shirts.

Demand for shirts increased, though. The potential income was hard to deny. I started saying yes more often. When I printed my first batch of mail order catalogs in 1993, I had five designs that I offered in two sizes. It was a nice sideline income and I didn't feel like I was doing anything wrong.

When I opened my record shop in 1995, my employee Kevin and I built a small T-shirt rack. I printed shirts in the storage room before and after hours and during lulls in business. It was a nice set up.

I made a few new designs and the rack plumped up. The six dollar white T-shirt became a staple of our local scene. Every kid in town had a couple. Over the years I added designs as they occurred to me. Sometimes people would suggest designs. I usually turned down their suggestions. If it was not something I'd personally wear, I probably would not print it.

By 2000, music sales began slipping. And T-shirt sales went up. I thought this was fucked up. People were willing to spend money on fashion but not the music. I generally ran my business like a music fan. I stocked items I could get behind, music I thought was important from bands I wanted to support.

T-shirts are an accessory, not nearly as important as the music itself. But declining sales had me reevaluating this approach. For the first time, I looked at my business from a financial perspective and saw I was on the road to failure. I knew I had to stop following my heart and cater to public demand. In retrospect, I should have closed the business, but I thought that music sales would return. (I also had no idea what else I could do for a living.) I figured I'd use the T-shirts to supplement my income until the music buying populace pulled their heads out of their asses.

So in spring of 2000, I began a campaign to save my business through bootleg merchandising. I did not feel good about it but I saw it as necessary. To make myself feel a little better, I only made designs for bands I liked, never bands with mass commercial appeal. It was my ethical compromise. In a matter of months, my design catalog expanded from about 25 designs to 120. The T-shirt rack swelled; my printed mail order catalog swelled. Income increased, but I still limped along.

From 2000 until 2007, I maintained my catalog of 120 designs. That was plenty, I thought. But music sales kept dropping and shirt sales continued to rise. I hated the trend but followed it. I renewed my T-shirt campaign with intensified cynicism.

I scoured my record collection for more images to turn into T-shirt designs. The band SSD released an album called *The Kids Will Have Their Say*, a powerful record with a powerful title. My jaded new mantra became, "The Kids Will Have Their T-shirts."

Fuck 'em. If they'd rather look like punk rockers than *be* punk rockers, I'll take their money. Fuck the shit out of these poseurs. My catalog of designs expanded to 225 images. I rebuilt my T-shirt rack to accommodate the new designs. My printed mail order catalog doubled in size. I raised the price of my shirts from six dollars to eight dollars and then to ten dollars. Much more money came in. Fashion money. It still was not enough to keep me afloat.

One summer evening in 2008, I was totaling up daily sales at the store. It was a pretty good day for a change. I thought about what I had sold over the counter that day: seventeen T-shirts, two vinyl records, and no CDs. The writing was on the wall. That was the moment I knew I had to close the store.

I realized that merchandise was the future and that music sales were out. I figured that if I again expanded my catalog and cut my overhead, I could make a good living from T-shirts alone. By my calculations, I could work fewer hours and double my money if I closed the store and opened a screen printing shop in a small, no frills warehouse.

I went home and told Ella. She was supportive, as always. In all the years of struggle, she never once asked me to close the shop and get a real job. Now she sweetly asked me if I was sure it was necessary; she knew the store meant a lot to me. In years past, it did mean a lot. But by 2008, it was like a dying pet. I just wanted to put it out of its misery and get on with my life. Yes, I told her, it is time. She was sad. She had emotional attachment to the place, too. Our first kiss was there.

With Ella behind my idea, I ran over the plans in my head a few times. This should work. I would have an easier work schedule, more money for our household, and more time for Ella. I had to do it. One by one, I called my four faithful employees, Sam, Pete, Pat, and Brian L, to tell them the news. Pete took it the worst. I asked them to keep it secret until I was ready to tell everyone else.

I secured a warehouse four and a half miles from my home. My commuting time would be cut to a third, another plus. My overhead dropped 80 percent.

On October 11, 2008, I publicly announced the store closing. I made a flyer with all the details and passed it out at the store's Saturday night concert. The concert-going crowd was in disbelief. They assumed the store would be around forever. At one point, I did, too. I wanted to run a record shop until I got wrinkly and old. But nothing lasts forever.

My last day in business was October 18, 2008. I sold, gave away or threw out everything but my screen printing stuff. The next day I set up shop at Unit 49-B.

Unit 49-B is about a quarter of the size of the record shop and is strictly utilitarian. There is no air conditioning, no telephone, and no Internet. I never put any decorations on the walls. Unlike the record store, I didn't want this place to be my second home. It was strictly for business. I only went there to work and I had no love for the work. It was a big step down in terms of comfort and emotional attachment. There would be none of either here.

At home, I set up an office in the living room. Ella and I bought our house in 2000, but in the eight years we were there, I rarely saw the place in the daytime. I was always at the store. It was odd to be home in the afternoon.

I liked my living room office. I could look out on our yard as I worked. I took orders over the computer, printed them the same day at the warehouse, and then dropped them off at the post office. It was the perfect set up. I ran it with efficiency. After years of juggling many balls at the record store, this was a piece of cake.

But there was one crucial flaw in my new business plan: Almost all the designs were unauthorized. It was a house of cards. Once in a while, a band would catch up with me.

Usually the bands were cool and we'd work out an agreement. A few groups were pissed off and asked me to stop. A lawyer representing two bands sent me a cease and desist letter. That scared me a little. But whenever a band asked me to stop bootlegging shirts, I would apologize and comply immediately. The crux: If enough bands complained, I'd be out of business. That never happened, but in theory it could have. The more designs I had, the better my chance for survival. It was a delicate balancing act.

And the money did not double as I had calculated. I still don't know why. In an attempt to remedy this situation, I cranked out more designs. I wanted to increase my catalog from 225 images to 400. By the time I got to about 300 images, I was out of ideas.

If I couldn't find an image for a band I liked, I'd just fabricate one. A lot of times people would say, "I've never seen that design before." Of course not, I just came up with it. These original creations were some of my most popular and I got a little satisfaction from this, but on the whole, screen printing was not emotionally rewarding work for me. It was just work.

The money was better than the record store, but not much better. The upside was I had a lot more time for Ella. Unfortunately, I didn't spend as much of it with her as I should have. I dug deeper into record collecting, chasing after more and more obscure pieces. I spent hours online doing research and chatting with collectors. My Internet radio show took up a lot of time. I took my beautiful wife for granted. I figured she'd always be there when I got done with my shit.

After moving out of our home, I kept the screen printing business running for several months but I grew to hate it. Under the circumstances, there was not much that I got pleasure from anymore. Therapy helped a lot. I thought I was getting better.

But one day at Unit 49-B, I totally broke down. The emotional weight of our separation and impending divorce caught me off guard and crushed me as surely as a boulder. I was in the middle of setting up for a printing session and the weight dropped on me without warning. I collapsed on the table and lost control. I fell apart. I couldn't do this anymore. I couldn't stay in Tampa.

In February 2013, I printed my last shirt and sold the business to a friend for a fraction of its value. I just wanted to be rid of it.

The guts of my bootleg T-shirt empire, Unit 49-B. Photo by Bob Suren.

WHERE: EGYPT AND ECUADOR

The first few months of the separation were a pressure cooker. Sleep was impossible. Each day began with my mantra, "Fuck," and ended with, "God damn it." Fuck. God damn it. Repeat.

I needed to somehow relax and enjoy myself. I thought a vacation would be a great idea. I was at my pointless, new, part time job, killing hours until I could go home, when an idea popped in my head: Egypt. I always wanted to go there. Ella and I talked about it a couple of times. We liked traveling and often discussed places we'd like to see. Egypt was on the wish list.

I had been selling my record collection for months and had money pouring in. How much could a trip to Egypt cost? I put down the pile of work I was supposed to be doing, logged onto the company computer, and researched airfare. It was easily affordable. It took me four seconds to decide to go.

I texted a friend from work: "I am going to Egypt!" He texted back: "Go for it. I am so fucking jealous." I left work early without telling anyone, went home, and bought my plane ticket.

That night I began doing research for my trip. I had ten days to prepare. Usually I would do the research before buying the ticket, but this was an act of whimsy. It felt great to be impetuous. For once, I had the money to do something outrageous. And planning the trip took my mind off of my misery for a while.

In therapy, I told Dr. R. that I was going on a vacation. He said that it was a positive move. He asked where I was going. Egypt, I told him, breaking a broad smile. He laughed. I asked him if I should tell Ella. I figured she'd be jealous and view this as a selfish move. Dr. R. told me that I deserved to relax and that I didn't have to tell Ella where I was going but that I should tell her I would be out of town for a while.

The night before I left, I had a small gathering at a café. I invited about twenty people to come hang out with me. About a dozen showed up. One of these was an exotic woman about half my age. I thought she was flirting with me, but she was just being friendly. The young woman asked me to pick up a souvenir for her. Yes, of course. We sat close. Our knees touched. I tried to imagine touching other parts of her, but Ella's face kept breaking into my thoughts. I still loved her and we were still married.

About midnight, I left the café. I walked the mile to the home I voluntarily left months earlier, to leave a note on the doorstep. The note read: "I am going out of town for a while. If you'd like to talk, please call me soon." Then I walked back to 203 to try to sleep. I had a cab coming in less than five hours.

After tossing and turning for a few hours, I got up and rechecked my backpack. I got dressed for the airport and logged onto the computer. Almost as soon as I logged on, I got an instant message from the exotic, young woman half my age. She wished me luck on the trip. We made plans to meet up when I returned so I could show her photos and give her the souvenir. The very moment we said goodbye, my phone rang. It was Ella.

"I got your note. Are you OK?"

"Not really..."

"Are you going to England?"

She assumed I was going to visit Patrick Lawlor in Worcester; he'd gone from being one of my best mail order customers to one of my best friends.

"No. I'm going to Egypt."

There was a long pause. I wondered what she was thinking. She probably thought I was full of shit or that I was planning something crazy.

"Wow," she said flatly.

I told her when I would be back and just then, I saw the cab pull up.

"The cab is here. I have to go. I love you forever."

"Goodbye."

Twenty hours and four planes later, I was in Cairo. Egypt is amazing but in my state of mind, it was difficult to enjoy. More than once, I found myself humbled and astounded, standing before some ancient monolith. I would turn to my side, expecting to see my wife and she wasn't there. Not having anyone to share the experience with was a damper.

At night, I would return to some luxury hotel room and freak out all night. I was half a world away from the love of my life, alone, laying in some giant, luxurious bed made for lovers. I felt like I was stranded on the moon.

In Alexandria, I had a room on the seventh floor. My balcony overlooked the Mediterranean Sea. I thought about jumping. Everything could be over in a few terrifying seconds. I leaned over the rail and considered it for a long time. Not tonight, I told myself. That was August.

In February, I took another trip for different reasons. Egypt was supposed to be about fun and adventure and clearing my head. I went to Ecuador looking for a new home.

I'd finished selling all of my records just before Christmas and I had a nice piece of change in my savings account. An online article said that Ecuador was an upcoming retirement spot. I was not quite ready to retire and I didn't have quite enough money to do so, but by my calculations, I could live in Ecuador for seven or eight years without working.

Of course, if I did move there, I would find a job to keep myself busy and to keep from depleting my savings. I did a bit of research and Ecuador seemed pretty great, particularly the city of Cuenca. Cuenca is considered the most beautiful city in Ecuador and the nation's cultural center. I planned to be in Cuenca on my forty-fourth birthday.

On my birthday, I was walking the hilly, cobblestone streets of Cuenca, enjoying the crisp weather and the dramatic architecture. The picturesque Tomebamba River roared behind me as I headed toward Calle Larga, one of the main streets in town. To my left, a radiant young woman sat on the steps of an art gallery. We caught eyes. She smiled warmly at me. I smiled back and kept walking. I took two more steps and said to myself, "What the hell are you doing? Go talk to her."

I walked toward her and she kept smiling. This was a good sign. Women do not usually smile as I approach them. I sat next to her on the steps and we exchanged names. Giovanna. A lovely name. It suited her.

She asked me if I'd like to see the gallery. I do like art, but I was not that interested. I did, however, want to spend more time with Giovanna. She led me into the gallery and locked the door behind her so that no one else could come in. It was just the two of us, locked in a three-story art gallery. She showed me around the gallery and explained each piece. I was not paying much attention to what she said.

When the tour concluded on the third floor, she took a seat by the window. I sat next to her and we talked. Not only was she beautiful, but she was beautifully dressed. I took a photo of her. It's a great one. We made plans for dinner. I kissed her comely cheek and said goodbye. She was still smiling. Cuenca on my birthday: Good call!

I stood in front of my hotel, waiting for Giovanna to arrive. I hoped she wouldn't stand me up. Two minutes after we were supposed to meet, she walked up, splendidly dressed and made up. She looked like a model. Over dinner, she told me she is an actress.

We walked several blocks to the finest restaurant in town. I ate there the day before. It is the perfect place for a date. Giovanna had never been there. She loved it.

We had a long talk over a long dinner. Such a charming woman she is. I guessed she was much younger than me. I didn't ask her age because I didn't want to tell her mine. Finally, she brought up the subject. At first I ignored her, but then she asked again.

"Well, today is my birthday…"

"Really? Why didn't you say?"

"Because I didn't want to tell you my age."

"How old are you?"

"Forty-four. Is that OK?"

"Yes. I don't mind."

"How old are you?"

"Twenty-two."

Dinner on my birthday with a beautiful actress half my age. This was much better than a night alone in 203.

After dinner, we sat on the steps of a cathedral, talking and watching people walk by. I asked her if I could kiss her. Only on the cheek, she said. I asked her if I could kiss her mouth. She shook her head.

"No. It's not right."

I'm not sure what she meant, but I didn't want to push it. I was pleased to be next to her. And her cheek was great for kisses. I gave her three.

I walked her home and returned to my hotel elated. Cuenca offered hope.

Cuenca, Ecuador, Feb. 2013. Photo by Bob Suren.

YOUNG WASTENERS
WE GOT WAYS LP
KICK N PUNCH RECORDS 2002

Cutter moved around a lot. She showed up at the record store one Halloween. She was dressed funny but not because it was Halloween. She always dresses funny.

At first people were like, "What the hell?" But then they talked to her and made friends. Cutter used to bring cookies and cakes to the record shop and pass them out. It's a good way to meet people. She dances silly. I like her. Ella likes Cutter, too. She's easy to like.

Cutter didn't drink. She does now, but not back then. I don't drink. Cutter and I formed a band with the only other two people in town who didn't drink. We called the band No Substance; it was Cutter's idea. I thought that was clever. I came up with a band logo and spray painted it on my drum set.

None of our songs were about abstinence from alcohol. The four of us just didn't drink and we wanted to play music together. It's too bad we never recorded anything because we had a few good songs.

Shortly after I met Cutter, she was lamenting being broke. Her mother's birthday was coming up and she wanted to get her a nice gift. She wanted to sell me the Young Wasteners album. I didn't have much money either, but someone gave me a camera tripod for Christmas and it was still in the box, unused. I traded the tripod for the album and we were both happy. Her mom liked the tripod, too.

When Ella and I separated, Cutter was one of the first people I called. She cried almost as hard as I did. She spent a lot of time with us. She thought we were a good couple. Cutter and I cried on the phone for an hour. She invited me to come live in a spare bedroom in Austin, Texas. She said she could help me find a job there, too. I kept this in the back of my mind.

Outter and Sam dancing by the T-shirts. Lower Found Area. Photographer unknown.

WHERE: THE INDEPENDENT

The Independent is a small bar and café a couple of streets from lonely 203. I did a lot of writing at the Independent. I also met a lot of friends there, just to hang out and be away from 203 for a while.

One night shortly after Ella and I split up, I was hanging out with my friend Keith when a gorgeous woman caught my eye. I moved in for a closer look. It was Ella. She was there with a friend, too. I went over and said hello. It was awkward, so I left. Man, did she look good that night.

Another night, June joined me at the Independent. She looked fantastic and was being a little flirty. I flirted right back. I had not felt this way since my first date with Ella eighteen years earlier. That was the night Ella stole my heart with a simple wink. I thought if June winked at me, I might have to marry her. We sat close. I brushed the blond hair from her face so I could get a better look at her eyes—and so I could touch her.

I winked at her. She winked back. I swooned.

In the parking lot we kissed like teenagers. The next time I saw her, she told me it was a mistake.

The Independent Bar and Café in Tampa. Photo by David Manuel

VARIOUS ARTISTS
A COMPILATION DEDICATED
TO TIM YOHANNAN LP
BOOTLEG 2000

Tim Yohannan, also known as Tim Yo, was one of the founders of *Maximum Rocknroll* magazine. Tim and a few other people started *Maximum Rocknroll* as a radio show in California in 1978. By 1982, the *Maximum* crew began publishing the magazine that would become loved by some, hated by others, but without a doubt crucial to the development of punk rock around the world.

I have not always agreed with Tim and have had a few minor beefs with *Maximum* over the years, but I am a big supporter. I have great respect for Tim's vision and dedication. *Maximum Rocknroll* is entirely non-profit and while it has struggled in recent times, in the good years, Tim funneled any money remaining at the end of the year to do-it-yourself projects. One year Tim rewarded me with one of these grants.

Tim died in 1998. The magazine and radio show continue in his absence, the way he would have wanted it. Both still operate in accordance to his guidelines, written and unwritten. Tim knew he was dying and wrote a manual for running *Maximum Rocknroll.*

My first contact with Tim was in 1991 after writing a whiny letter to the record reviewer who gave my record a bad review. While I was at work, Tim called and left a sarcastic, bitter, and nasty message on my answering machine. Nice to meet you, too, sir.

That was Tim: Guns blazing always. No punches pulled. He never backed down on anything. Some say he was hard headed. Some say he was narrow-minded. I say he was fearlessly dogmatic. Like him or not, you had to respect Tim.

In 1993, Tim called me again. This time I was home and he was far more cordial. But it was a business call. He asked me if I wanted to reserve ad space in the magazine each month. It was a business move, but I was flattered. I didn't know I was on Tim's radar. I said yes and then Tim told me I was doing good work and to keep it up. It was a nice pat on the back.

By 1997, my record distribution business was doing well. It seemed like it could go pretty far. I was networking with a lot of people in California. Many of them felt like friends. I decided it was time to take a trip out west to meet some of these people and maybe learn more about the record business.

I called Tim and told him I was coming for a visit. He invited me over to *Maximum Rocknroll* to see how they operated and to check out their legendary record collection.

The *Maximum Rocknroll* record collection is a vast archive of nearly every punk rock record ever made. Over the years, a few pieces have been stolen but it is as complete as can be. Tim was a voracious record hunter. He wanted everything. Even in the days leading up to his death, he clung to a long want list of items—most of which were so obscure I'd never even heard of them. Every few years, Tim mailed me an updated version of his list. I had two of the items but would not part with them. Now and then, Tim would ask me if I still had them and wanted to sell or trade. Sorry, Tim.

My friend John picked me up at the airport in San Francisco. I dropped off my pack at his apartment and we went out to see the sights—specifically record stores. I told John that I was going to *Maximum Rocknroll* to check out the collection and that he should come along, too.

John and I were in Epicenter, a record store started in the late 1980s with funding from *Maximum Rocknroll*, searching for vinyl. John found one or two things, but I was striking out. To the right of me, I noticed a middle-aged man with a fat stack of albums. He was digging through the bins at a feverish rate, plopping piece after piece on his pile. He must have had 30 albums and seemed rather pleased with his spoils. John nudged me and said, "That's Tim Yohannan."

"That's Tim Yohannan?" I thought. He looked like a grandpa. His hair was gray and thin. He had dark circles under his eyes and bad teeth. And he was wearing what I can only describe as a dingy "old man sweater."

I stepped over to introduce myself. Tim smiled widely and chuckled a little. He noticed that I didn't have any records. I told him nothing caught my eye.

"I'm finding plenty," he replied. Then he looked at his watch and headed for the sales counter. When he finished checking out, he told me that I could come by *Maximum*

Rocknroll in a couple of hours and wrote down the address for me.

Two hours later, we were standing in *Maximum Rocknroll*, overwhelmed by the Great Wall of Vinyl. The collection is L-shaped. It runs the entire length of one long wall and around the corner, four or five rows high. Just seeing the mass was an overwhelming experience. Tim told me how many records there were but I don't remember. It was an absurd figure. Tim told us that we could have a few hours to look and that he had work to do. John and I thanked him and started exploring the Library of Congress of Punk Rock.

I wanted to look at everything. Not possible. Not in one day, at least. I started with the singles and flipped through them rapidly. After two hours, I was somewhere in the "D" section. There was no way I could see it all. I began skipping around the shelves looking for specific items that I knew I'd never see elsewhere. I chanced across a few of my own releases. It was very satisfying knowing they were housed in this vital archive.

John was running around without a real plan, hunting records as they occurred to him. *Maximum* had them all. John brought along a few blank tapes. Tim graciously let John make copies of several rare records. I had not thought to bring tapes.

While John and I giddily perused Punk Rock Nirvana, Tim was busy training his replacement, a young woman named Jen. Tim knew he didn't have much time left.

In addition to running *Maximum Rocknroll*, he held a day job in the shipping department at the University of California. He ran the *Maximum* Empire after work for no pay, just a lot of bullshit and criticism. A year after I met Tim, almost to the day, he died. One of my record business buddies in California called to tell me. I knew he was dying, but it still took me aback.

Tim was not a very sentimental guy. He did not want any special fanfare when he was gone. Nonetheless, pages have been written about him and even a few songs have been recorded about him—one not so flattering. And in 2000, a bootleg album was released as a tribute to Tim with some of his old favorites.

VARIOUS ARTISTS
FRANK FOREVER LP
BURN BRANDON RECORDS 2003

Burn Brandon was a community-run magazine and record label based out of my record shop. Around 1999, a group of bored teenagers was hanging around the store telling me that they were bored teenagers. It was, "This town sucks," and all that stuff that teenagers all over the world say about their towns, decade after decade. I asked them what they'd like to do, what would alleviate their boredom. One of them said he'd like to start a magazine.

Smart kid. I liked him. I liked most of the kids who hung out at the shop, but especially this one. He could have said a lot of things but he said something positive, something creative, something potentially galvanizing. I agreed to help.

I had a photocopier that they could use. I told them, "You guys write the stuff and I'll print it up." Furthermore, I had a degree in journalism and had previously published eight issues of my own music magazine. I would help with technical stuff and offer advice when needed.

We held a meeting at the record shop, inviting anyone who wanted to be part of the new project. Eight or ten people showed up. Of those, maybe two contributed to the first issue. But the ball was rolling. An idea was planted.

At that first meeting, a major order of business was voting on a name for the project. There were silly suggestions that I am glad did not get many votes. I think it was the smart kid, the one I liked, who came up with the name *Burn Brandon*. It made a statement; I loved it.

We also laid down some other tenets at that first meeting. The magazine would be free and we would never accept advertising. To fund the magazine, we'd ask for donations. That was how the first two issues were financed. But donations were hard to come by and we were shooting for increased press runs, more frequent publishing, and, above all, longevity. By the third issue, we'd established a practice of holding benefit concerts to pay for the magazine. Usually one good concert would finance an issue. Sometimes there was leftover money for the next issue.

We agreed that the magazine should have a strong local focus. We reasoned it was more vital to write about the music in our own town than music in California. Other people were writing about that music. Nobody was writing about us. Or ever would.

We agreed that the magazine would not be used for personal attacks against individuals. We did not want it to become a gossip rag. No slander, no rumors. We tried to take the high ground. And that was pretty much it.

Eventually we expanded *Burn Brandon* into a record label. Like the magazine, the records were financed by donations and benefit concerts and were given away, never sold. Between 1999 and 2008, the Burn Brandon collective made twenty issues of the magazine, a CD of local bands, three 7" records, and the highlight of our efforts, the *Frank Forever* album.

Now, you may be asking, who is Frank and why did he get a record named after him? Frank Vagnozzi was the singer and guitarist of the Reckless Deerhunters, a staple of the local music scene. Frank was a big, funny, curious, supportive guy who everyone liked. Frank passed away in 2003, a tremendous blow to our crowd. The album was already in the works when Frank died, but it had no title or cover art yet. It became obvious that the record had to be dedicated to him.

The first time I met Frank, I couldn't tell if he was brimming with enthusiasm or if he was trying to pull a practical joke on me. I had been doing free Sunday matinee concerts at my record store for a year. My booking policy was simple. Bring me something to listen to and if I liked your band, you got a show.

So, one day I was sitting at my desk, wondering where the customers were and two guys walked in. There was a big guy, Frank, and a sinewy guy, George. I'd never seen them before and, as is my nature, I was distrustful of strangers. At the record store, people were always trying to get me to do favors for them. Usually these favors were way beyond my possibilities, like, "Hey, can you get us signed to a record label?" Probably not, but would you like to buy a bootleg Ramones shirt?

Frank introduced himself and George. George didn't do any talking but he smiled. Frank was smiling so brightly that I immediately became suspicious. What the hell did this guy want?

"Hi, I'm Frank and this is George. We're in a band and we'd like to play here." Enormous smile. Slight pause while I tried to size them up. I couldn't size them up.

"Do you have a tape I could listen to?" I asked flatly.

"Yes, right here," Frank said, handing me the tape in a way that was almost ceremonial. He slightly bowed his head as he held the tape out for me. I wondered if he had been an altar boy.

The tape label read, "Reckless Deerhunters," in pen, in Frank's printing that I came to see a lot of over the next few years.

"We're called the Reckless Deerhunters," Frank said, just in case I couldn't read. He was still smiling like a kook. Was this guy fucking with me?

I put the tape on, not knowing what to expect but thinking it would probably be bad and—it was pretty good. I looked at Frank and George; they were grinning and bopping around a little. I swear I saw Frank elbow George in the ribs in the manner of, say, the Three Stooges or Fred Flintstone. Then it hit me. Their name is really funny.

The next song came on. Frank told me it was called, "Things to do When You're Home Alone." The lyrics were a random laundry list of banality. This made me smile. But I still couldn't tell if these guys were setting me up for something. Frank and George were clearly enjoying listening to their own tape. I decided these guys were OK with me. Harmless goofs.

The band got a show and they were good. The local teenagers took to them. They became a draw, entertaining one crowd after another for the next several years. (After Frank's passing, the other members kept it going for five more years as a tribute to him.)

Frank and Scott, the drummer, were older—older than me by a few years—but they never thought it beneath them to play free concerts in the storage room of a record store for a bunch of people half their age or less. They seemed to relish each moment, especially Frank, who just got so absolutely wrapped up in playing. They used to play a cover of "Baba O'Riley" by the Who, that while not technically as proficient, was packed with such emotion that it trumps the original. To this day I cannot hear that song without seeing Frank hitting the bridge, "Don't cry, don't raise your eye, it's only teenage wasteland." Despite the lyrics, this brings a tear to my eye every time I hear it.

Like all people, Frank had some demons. We talked about these sometimes. Once as we were eating at the Subway restaurant across the street from the record shop, Frank told me that he was seeing a therapist. The therapist asked Frank, "What makes you happy?" Frank said music. The therapist told Frank to play music as much as possible. And he did. I think Frank would have liked to have done more with music, but he took it as far as he possibly could. I remember at least once when Frank asked me what else he could be doing to further the band. It is a question all musicians ask at some time and I'll be damned if I know. I had no good answer for him.

Frank's tastes were far more varied than mine. He found merit in many things I glossed over or would not even consider. He looked for the good in everything he heard. He had not a jaded bone in his body. Or at least his ears.

Frank was known for watching every band at every show. While a lot of people would hang out in the parking lot, leaving bands to play to meager crowds, Frank was always up front and always smiling. Afterward, he would find something nice to say to the group, usually something very specific. He paid attention to music. I could never muster his enthusiasm. I only saw him walk out on one band, not because they were bad—Frank liked amateurs—but because they were a bunch of jerks.

Frank was often between jobs but I could always tell when he got paid because he'd be in the store stacking up CDs. He'd blow huge chunks of his paycheck on music, always with a smile. I used to thank him for buying music and he would in turn thank me for selling it to him.

When Frank had no money, he would hang around the record shop begging me to play things and asking questions. I could not keep up with him. Before I could answer one question, he'd have two or three more. Frank was a sponge. He wanted to know it all and hear it all.

He was impossible not to like. Once he told me that he thought a particularly stoic person did not like him. I told him that was not true. After Frank died, that person called me to say how much he missed him. See, Frank, everybody liked you.

After Frank passed away, we held a meeting about this album. We'd already begun the planning but had not raised any money yet. We quickly determined that the record had to be dedicated to Frank, the smiling diplomat of our music scene.

I contacted all the companies involved in the manufacturing process and explained the situation, making sure to note that the record would be given away, never sold. All of them were kind enough to offer deep discounts to the project. Thanks again to Imprint, Dorado Press, Frankford Wayne Record Mastering, and United Record Pressing. I made sure that all of them got copies of the record when it came out.

Six benefit shows raised enough money to make 600 copies of the album. Copies of the record have made it to Japan, Australia, Europe, South America, and all over the U.S. I made sure copies got to two of Frank's musical heroes, Jello Biafra and Henry Rollins. One song was played on an internationally syndicated radio program. My tireless sales rep at United Record Pressing tells me her copy is hanging in her office in Nashville.

I consider this the most important project I have ever worked on. Frank's on the cover.

VARIOUS ARTISTS
GRITO SUBURBANO LP
PUNK ROCK DISCOS 1982

By 2003, Murder-Suicide Pact, the band that I started in late 1997 was running on fumes. We barely practiced anymore. We had not written a new song in years and getting everyone to agree to play a show was difficult. My creative outlet had become an albatross. Or maybe a dead horse—which one is worse? It was definitely some sort of cumbersome animal. Anyhow, I reckoned it was time to call it quits before we became pathetic or started hating each other. I scheduled a final show for March.

We had a couple of "last shows" before, but this was really it for me. I was already thinking of new people to play with and saving new song ideas in a ratty, orange folder. A couple of weeks before our scheduled finale, I got an email from a Brazilian record label asking if we'd like to make a new record. I told the label thank you, but we didn't have any new songs and that we'd be breaking up soon.

Alex, the label guy, said, "That's too bad. But before you break up, you should do a tour of Brazil." Hmmm... That got my attention. Alex said that if we could buy our own plane tickets, he'd arrange everything else. In all the years I'd been playing music it was the sweetest offer I ever received. A foreign vacation with my friends—and we got to rock every night. At our next band practice, I ran the details by the guys and they were in. I got back to Alex and told him to book it.

At our scheduled "last show," I told the audience that we were going to hang around a little longer and they cheered. Then I told them we'd be representing Brandon, Florida in the Southern Hemisphere and they cheered some more. We usually played shows for no money, but to finance this trip, we did a series of paid gigs. I think it took thirteen gigs for us to buy our four plane tickets.

In November, we arrived in São Paulo with our guitars, a snare drum, and cymbals. The rest of the gear would be provided for us each night. We'd be doing five shows with a Brazilian band called Social Chaos. Tour manager Alex and Borella from Social Chaos picked us up at the airport in two small cars, the tour vehicles. Eight people and gear in two small cars. It was cozy.

Before the tour started, I asked Alex if he could book us with some of my favorite Brazilian bands. I rattled off about six or eight bands, not knowing if they were still around. The one I was most interested in was Olho Seco, the godfathers of Brazilian hardcore punk, founded in 1980.

My favorite Olho Seco songs are their recordings on a compilation, *Grito Suburbano*. These songs are incredibly visceral. Most impressive are singer Fabio Sampaio's snarling vocals. Fabio commands complete attention with terse, urgent diatribes set to a pounding beat. I have no idea what he is saying, but holy shit, he sounds serious and furious. I rank Fabio among the best of the best.

While Alex was impressed with my knowledge of Brazilian hardcore, he told me that most of the bands I wanted to play with were no longer active and the one that was still going was difficult to work with. Unfortunately, Olho Seco was deceased. However, Alex told me that Fabio owned a record store and that we could visit it. Awesome. I told Alex that I intended to wear a Olho Seco T-shirt on stage every single night, a promise that I kept.

The shows were great. Each night was crazier than the one before. In São Bernardo, the sound man pulled the plug after the second song because he was worried about the mayhem. Alex talked him into letting us finish, promising to pay for any damage.

I fell off the high stage, landing on my right elbow. The fall left me with bone chips and permanent nerve damage. (Alex couldn't pay for that!) After the show, a guy told me in labored English, "Your band is like wrestling!" I took that as a compliment. I told our bassist, a huge Hulk Hogan fan, and he was thrilled.

I got shocked by an ungrounded microphone in São Paulo. We couldn't get the shock to go away, so I played with a shirt wrapped around the mic and tried to keep my mouth from touching the screen. Every time I connected with the screen, *zap!* I had a little burn on my lower lip for a day or two.

In Bauru, I dove off the stage onto a table, shattering it on impact. The audience ran around, shaking broken table legs in their hands. I think the club owner was mad about that.

And in Assis, an errant stage diver elbowed me in the face. (I finished the tour and flew home with a shiner!) After this show, a reporter asked me about our band. I told him that we were from Florida. He wrote that down. When he asked me if there were any other good bands from Florida, I mentioned a small, local band of nice teenagers named Lawnmowers Gone Awry. I told him they were the best band in the United States and he wrote it down. I don't know if that ever made it to print, but I still chuckle thinking about it.

At the final concert in Londrina, a small teenager, totally decked out in punk rock garb, stood directly in front of me, rattling his fists in enjoyment. I figured him for about 110 pounds. I picked him up over my head and tossed him into the audience like a beach ball. The audience tossed him back to me and we played catch with this kid for a few songs. He really seemed to like it. After this show, a breathy, young woman ran up to me and with a little difficulty said, "Your music is perfect." That's as good as you can get, right? Better than "like wrestling."

Between shows, we visited local landmarks, outdoor markets, a waterfall, and lots of shops. Of course, the shop I was most interested in was Decontrol Discos, Fabio's store. Alex and I walked in and there he was, Fabio Sampaio, the voice and face of Brazilian punk.

Alex made the introductions. Fabio spoke almost no English so Alex translated for us. I expressed what a big fan I was and Fabio smiled. I embarrassed myself by trying to sing Olho Seco's most famous song, "Nada." Fabio laughed at that. Some other guy in the shop looked at me like I was a total moron but I didn't care. I had Alex explain to Fabio that I would like his permission to reissue some early Olho Seco material on my record label. Fabio nodded and shook my hand, but nothing ever came of this.

When Alex explained that I wore an old, shitty Olho Seco shirt on stage every night, Fabio arched his eyebrows, reached behind the sales counter and tossed me a new Olho Seco shirt. Alex snapped a picture of us standing together, holding up the shirt. I have a wide smile. It was a big moment for me.

I had Alex invite Fabio to our gig that night and then the two of them had a long discussion. Alex explained that

Fabio has an inner ear disorder from playing loud music for so many years. Now if he is around loud music, the disorder causes him to lose his equilibrium; he gets dizzy and falls down. Fabio is no longer able to play music or go to gigs. Even the music in his record shop was playing at a whispering volume.

Fabio and I shook hands and exchanged contact info. It was truly inspiring to meet the guy who not only made a ton of crucial music, but who was instrumental in the development of punk rock in South America. Legend.

We returned from Brazil in high spirits, especially me. We got back to work, practicing, and playing more often and writing new songs for the next ten years.

Me and Fabio from Olho Seco in his record store, Decontrol Discos, 2003. Photo by Alex Buchos.

VARIOUS ARTISTS
LET THEM EAT JELLYBEANS LP
ALTERNATIVE TENTACLES 1981

Some of the first punk rock songs I heard were culled from this excellent compilation and put on a fantastic mix tape that circulated among my friends for about a year. I never found out who made the original mix tape, but we all got copies. You can imagine how excited I was to find this album. But for some reason, I stole it.

I had never shoplifted before. It was only four dollars and I had plenty of money in my pocket. It was so easy to do, too. The record store I stole it from was a jumbled mess. It was a small building that was someone's house at one time. All of the rooms were jammed with records in no particular order.

A week or two earlier, I saw a rare record, the Nuclear Crayons 12", there but didn't have enough money, so I stashed it in the back of a box in a dark corner. I figured it would still be there by the time I had the money for it. This was a common practice in this particular record store. So, when I finally went back to the hiding spot, it was gone. I don't know if someone else bought it or if it got found and re-hidden, but I could not find it anywhere. Then I found *Jellybeans* and my eyes popped out. I never saw one before but I knew most of the songs.

I pulled the money out of my pocket, looked at it, and then stuffed it back in. I slipped the album into my backpack and walked out. The bored sales clerk didn't even notice me leave. The store got so little business, I think the owner just zoned out most of the time.

I always felt bad about this. Seven years later, I returned to town with the intention of spending a lot of money in the store as a way of making good on my crime. Of course, the right thing to do would have been to confess to the owner and just give him four dollars but I wasn't quite up for that. My plan was to make a large purchase and wash away my sins. But when I returned, the store was gone. Out of business. I felt partially responsible.

Years later when I was running my own record store, I caught two shoplifters. One, I kicked in the face a few times. The other I choked and screamed at. I pointed a loaded gun at another guy I suspected of shoplifting. In hindsight, I think that guy was innocent. I have been known to overreact.

Anyhow, that was not the last time I shoplifted, but it was the only time I ever took a record.

When business got bad at my record store, I was barely making enough money to get to and from work. It was pitiful. I resorted to shoplifting food almost every day from a local grocery store. If I didn't steal, I would not have been able to eat. Shoplifting my lunch helped keep me in business for an extra year or two. But then one day I realized that stealing is fucked. I would not want to be stolen from and I never did it again. And I lost a lot of weight.

VARIOUS ARTISTS
WE CAN'T HELP IT IF WE'RE FROM FLORIDA 7"
DESTROY RECORDS, 1983

I can't tell you how important this record is. Not just to me, but to the entire state of Florida (the punks, at least). At one time—and for many—it seemed that punk rock was from England, New York, and California. But as most now know, it was and is everywhere, continuing to spread and evolve. Punk caught on in different places at different times. The various interpretations betray a certain local color. (And this is something I truly love about the milieu.)

And so this record was and is the true calling card for the state of Florida. It was not the first Florida punk record— not even close in that race—but it is the one that called attention to the Sunshine State's nascent hardcore scene. This record was, for many, a first taste of Gator Punk. It is a sort of Whitman's Sampler of Florida circa 1983. The bands on it are Hated Youth, Sector 4 (both from Tallahassee), Morbid Opera (from Fort Lauderdale), Rat Cafeteria (from Tampa), and Roach Motel (from Gainesville.)

Destroy Records was run by the guys in Roach Motel. They were instrumental in making hardcore happen in Florida. Roach Motel was a hard-working band. They put out the first Florida hardcore record. They published thirteen issues of rowdy *Destroy* magazine. They put on numerous gigs. And they networked like crazy, drawing genre-defining touring bands like Black Flag, Dead Kennedys, Channel 3, the Necros, and Negative Approach to the state.

And of course, they masterminded this splendid record featuring five bands, all very different in style, yet all part of the same thing. Let's just say that you need this one under your belt. And if you don't already have it, you should find a copy or someone to copy it for you. It has been a regular blaster for me for many years. It strikes me as fresh, vital, and earnest, all this time later.

One of my favorite memories of this record is listening to it with my friend Chris at his house, sitting on his bed and trying to figure out who the hell these bands were. He broke out his acoustic guitar and quickly played an approximation of the three Hated Youth songs while I attempted to sing the lyrics in time to his frenetic strumming. It was not easy. It was the first time I ever tried to play music. I went home and told my parents that I started a band. They were quizzical, so I sang the song, "Army Dad," to them. Then they were disgusted. Hardcore rules.

THE EPILOGUE

Over three decades, music went from an interest to a passion to a fulfilling career to just a job. By the end it was a claustrophobic pigeonhole that I had to escape. I wanted to see what else the world had to offer.

I hoped that Ella and I could get back together but each day my hope grew colder and dustier. In the meanwhile, things heated up with June. She looked like my new hope. I courted her daily with phone calls and emails and in time she responded flirtatiously.

Our short time together was unpredictable and fun. Late one night after dinner and a party, she dragged me on a dance floor for a few minutes and then wanted to go to the beach. Her whims were always exciting and I always went along with whatever she wanted to do.

We were in my car, cracking each other up, driving to the beach. After some great laugh, the mood changed; she became still and silent. Following a pause, she spoke in a low, even tone. She spilled a long monologue, telling me all the things she admired about me. She said wonderful things that I had not heard in a long time, things I needed to hear. She was sincere and it touched me greatly. I don't remember another time that words felt so good.

She concluded her monologue by saying, "I love you." I didn't see that coming. And even though it felt premature, I told her the same. It was the best night of my year.

Back at 203, a packet of divorce papers was waiting under my doormat.

Five days later, Ella joined me at 203 and we filled out the papers together. It was unreal seeing the end of our relationship in black and white. As we drove to the public notary, I begged her again not to go through with this but she said it was too late.

I cried the entire time at the notary. Then Ella dropped me off at 203 and took the papers directly to the courthouse. I crashed on my bed and wailed. It felt like a vital piece of my body had been torn away and I was bleeding to death. I still loved her. I called June.

I stayed on the phone with June for about an hour. She comforted me and told me that things were going to be OK. When I was calm, she said, "Good night, sweet thing," and we hung up.

For months I had been planning to leave the country and start over in Costa Rica. Even though I'd never seen the place, I figured it had to be better than the bad memories of 203. My flight was in thirteen days. I began my planning before June and I got closer. I was conflicted but decided I still had to go. We'd talked about her joining me there, but that didn't happen. The phone call the day of the divorce papers was the last warmth she gave me. She stopped taking my calls and didn't attend my going away party.

Nineteen days after June said she loved me and thirteen days after signing divorce papers, I flew to Costa Rica alone with just a backpack of clothing, my laptop, and a small camera. It was all I owned.

My house was in an isolated area without a name near the Pacific. The dirt road the house was on had no name, either. The second day I was in Costa Rica, I bought a cell phone. My first call was to June.

She was avoiding me but I didn't know why. Since she didn't recognize my new number, she picked up on the second ring. I caught her off guard and asked her to please explain what she was thinking. Her two-sentence response left me with a lot of questions. I wanted some closure but instead she hung up on me. I still can't believe how much that hurt.

The house was beautiful but in the middle of nowhere. I had a lush, tropical yard full of vibrant flowers, coconut trees, palms, and banana trees. There were toucans, parrots and hummingbirds. There were monkeys and coatimundis, a relative of the raccoon with a long, pointy snout. There were boa constrictors and other snakes I couldn't identify. And millipedes everywhere.

I had a swimming pool. My bedroom balcony overlooked the pool. The guest room balcony overlooked raw jungle. I had cheap domestic help who did all the yard work and cleaned the house. It was a posh bachelor pad in the jungle that nobody ever saw but me.

I spent days at the beach or wandering jungle trails. I climbed mountains and trees. I took lots of photos. I figured out how the buses ran and visited the nearest civilization almost daily for groceries and yoga classes and tattered paperbacks. The bus stop was a tree a couple of miles from my house. Stand under the tree and wait for the bus.

I didn't sleep much. My nights were divided between wishing Ella would call me home and wondering what the hell June was thinking.

I started writing a new book with many short chapters that read like a journal. Here is a bit of it.

Chapter 43

Sweet June,

Last night I think I finally got over Ella. It was like reaching a long finish line. There was a clear break and a long, good cry and then relief. I'm sorry to bother you. You're the one I tell these things to. You have been so important to me. Thank you for everything. The last time I saw incredible you, we were inches away from falling in love. If you need me, that is where I'll be. I hope you are OK.

Bob

Of course, June didn't respond to that letter. The time alone did help me find some peace with losing Ella and June though there are still lots of things that I miss about both.

I spent 182 days in Central America. I used the jungle bachelor pad as a home base and branched out to explore much of Costa Rica as well as parts of Nicaragua, Guatemala, and Panama. The experiences should have been richer but I was dampened. It was bittersweet.

I was looking for a new home but nowhere seemed right. I gave it my best shot but it looked like I'd never find happiness in Central America. My friend Cutter again encouraged me to try life in Austin, Texas.

Without knowing a thing about Austin, I bought a one-way ticket and arrived on Dec. 5, 2013, a cold, bleak morning. It was great to see her friendly face at the airport. Her hug was the best I'd had in months. But the drab day had me wondering if Austin was a good choice.

She showed me the room I could stay in. I dropped my bags, laid down on the bare mattress, and cried for a couple of hours. Then I got up, unpacked and showered and she showed me the town. I started feeling better. That night she introduced me to some of her friends at a restaurant and that's when things started getting good. I hope to be here for a while.

THANK YOU

Shane Hinton, Sam, Pete, John and Sue Watson, Pat, Brian L., Rob and Cathy Sexton, Brian R., Kevin, Bob White, Kyle Stone, Christine Claybrook-Lumsden, Ward and Kim Young, Joe Biel, Elly Blue, and Meggyn Pomerleau at Microcosm, David Manuel, Tesco Vee, Chris BCT, Ami Lawless, Jeff Nelson, Al Quint, V. Vale, the 113-H family, and everyone who was there.

Me on the mic with Murder-Suicide Pact, last night of business at Sound Idea.
Photo by Kyle Stone.

SUBSCRIBE TO EVERYTHING WE PUBLISH!

Do you love what Microcosm publishes?

Do you want us to publish more great stuff?

Would you like to receive each new title as it's published?

Subscribe as a BFF to our new titles and we'll mail them all to you as they are released!

$10-30/mo, pay what you can afford. Include your t-shirt size and month/date of birthday for a possible surprise! Subscription begins the month after it is purchased.

microcosmpublishing.com/bff

...AND HELP US GROW YOUR SMALL WORLD!